IMAGES
of Wales

ELY COMMON TO CULVERHOUSE CROSS

The Dusty Forge – a stop along the way.

IMAGES
of Wales

ELY COMMON TO CULVERHOUSE CROSS

Compiled by
Nigel Billingham and Stephen K. Jones

TEMPUS

First published 1999
Copyright © Nigel Billingham and Stephen K. Jones, 1999

Tempus Publishing Limited
The Mill, Brimscombe Port,
Stroud, Gloucestershire, GL5 2QG

ISBN 0 7524 1197 7

Typesetting and origination by
Tempus Publishing Limited
Printed in Great Britain by
Midway Clark Printing, Wiltshire

Front cover: Ely Hospital staff in the mid-1920s (see p. 49).

Ely Station, 25 August 1959. A 0-6-0 pannier tank, No. 6435, is seen hauling the 5.43 p.m. train to Pontypridd. Note the original stone arch in the middle of the road bridge.

Contents

The Hathaway family, (mother, uncles and grandparents of Una McElveen). Left to right, standing at the back: Ernest and Jack. Front row standing: Anne (born 16 August 1900 and mother of Una) with Bill in front. Seated is Albert John Hathaway, with Jim between him and his wife Mary Jane (*née* Draper), then Bob and last on right seated is George. Albert and Mary Jane Hathaway married in 1885. Mary Jane was the daughter of Henry Draper who lived in Mill Road with his wife and six children (recorded in the 1881 census). He was employed as a stoker at the paper mill with place of birth given as Calne in Wiltshire.

Una McElveen with husband Gerald on left and Arthur Harrison, taken during the launch of his book on the history of Ely Methodist Church in 1974.

Foreword

I have lived in Ely all my life, as have my mother and grandmother's families before me. I enjoyed going to the Ely History Group meetings, run by Stephen and Nigel, and was particularly excited when one evening they showed the 1881 Census Returns for Ely and I found the names of my mothers' ancestors. My grandmother, Mary Jane Draper, lived with her family in Mill Road. She married my grandfather Albert John Hathaway in Cardiff on the 26 November 1885. My grandfather worked on many public works such as the Severn Tunnel, Brecon Reservoir, Porthkerry Viaduct and Swansea Docks. As I look at the family photograph, I realize that 'Ern' was the only one to follow Granddad in public works. He worked on the sewerage works in Yorkshire and married and settled there. Jack and Jim worked in Ely Hospital, Bill in Ely Brewery, George lost an arm in the First World War, after which, I suppose, he was unemployable, but Mr Palmer of Palmer's Nurseries always saw that there was something for him to do. Bob died young. My mother worked in Chivers Jam Factory and also for a time in the sewing room at Ely Hospital and I remember an incident one day when she didn't take her hand away quick enough from the machine and ended up sewing her hand as well! Fortunately it was not serious. With all these sons, only one son was born to the next generation, so sadly the Hathaway name will end with my cousin Colin.

I only remember my grandparents living at 6 Dyfrig Rd. It was and still is a lovely old house. I remember Mr Reagan telling me that when he was building the houses, someone said to him 'What do you think you are building there – A church?'. My grandparents were a lovely couple. As a young child I didn't like 'cooked dinners' and Gran would always give me money to go and buy a banana at the corner shop (much against my mother's wishes!). This was of course before the war – you couldn't get bananas during the war. My parents lived at several addresses including a house (now no more) which was next to the White Lion in Mill Road and owned by a Mrs Price. When Gran died, we moved into 6 Dyfrig Road so that my mother could look after Granddad. I remember him sitting in his wooden armchair beside the old fashioned range. In the corner cupboard he used to keep a bottle of Ely Ale and a tin of Kendal biscuits. My brother, Eric, was always allowed a sip of the beer but I was only allowed a Kendal biscuit! Granddad used to give me a shilling on my birthday – I suppose that was a lot of money then. Granddad died in June 1942. Both grandparents are buried in St Mary's churchyard. I used to walk or cycle up there regularly to tend the grave.

The nearest the war came to us was when a high explosive bomb fell in the garden of 28 Riverside Terrace. Quite a bit of damage was caused to our house by the blast and debris. After the raid we were standing at the gate when Mr Hurley the coalman came towards us absolutely covered in mud – he had fallen into the crater left by the bomb! St David's parish hall, in Clark Street, was taken over by the army and lorries used to come along to collect and deliver stores. All the drivers were very kind to us children but there was a 'special one' called Tom who was particularly kind to us, I suppose he had children of his own at home. Our parents didn't have to worry about us talking and playing with the men and sometimes we were allowed up into the cab when they 'moved up the queue'. As children during the war we found this really exciting.

Anyone my age would remember the floods in Ely. When one was threatened my father used to put sandbags across our front gate and pack some against the front door. Once this was done his next job would be to go over to Hedley Thomas (the chemist in Mill Road) to help him lift everything out of reach of the water as his shop was always one of the first to be flooded. The floods never came into our house in my lifetime but whenever we stripped the walls we could see the water mark well up the wall where it had reached in earlier days.

School for me started in Herbert Thompson, then Ely Council (now Millbank) and finally Howard Gardens High School. I worked for some time in the office of Stephen Treseder & Son. During all this time I spent most of my spare time at Ely Methodist church. The church has always been a very important part of life. Gerald and I were married in 1952. We have two children Eileen, who married Chris and Stephen who married Monica and have five lovely grandchildren. We continued to work at the church in the Sunday School and Youth Club etc. When the children were old enough I worked in Ely Hospital and worked there for twenty years. I really loved my work there. It is so sad that the hospital is no more, but there are many happy memories and it is lovely when I meet people who used to live there. They are so pleased to see you and that you recognize and speak to them. Gerald and I still keep very active in the church (we now attend Wesley Methodist in Canton) and community life.

Having enjoyed Stephen and Nigel's previous book on Ely I was thrilled to be asked to write this foreword to their new book and give an account of my own family history in Ely. It has brought back memories of what living in Ely really means. We have lived here all our lives in Ely and we love it.

Una McElveen

The late Revd Mary Evans at the launch of the first Ely book, December 1996. Left to right: Steve Jones, Revd Mary Evans, Revd R.H. Morgan, Nigel Billingham.

Introduction

This is the second book in the *Archive Photographs* Series covering the Ely, Caerau and Michaelston–super-Ely area of Cardiff. As the title, Ely Common to Culverhouse Cross, suggests this book aims to take the reader on a journey beginning at Ely Common (Victoria Park), travelling along Cowbridge Road East, over Ely Bridge along the main road (Cowbridge Road (West)) through Ely and completing the journey at Culverhouse Cross. It is by no means a strictly linear progression, as detours will be made on the way to both the north and south of the main road to look at people and places of interest.

A reader with intimate knowledge of this area of Cardiff will perhaps be surprised that the book begins at Victoria Park; an area which seems other than its proximity, to have little association with Ely. However before the official opening of Victoria Park in 1897 the park had been referred to in council minutes as Ely Park. Previous to this, and until Canton began to expand westwards, the whole area was in the countryside and was known as Ely Common or Ely Moors.

It was on the 8 July 1878 that the Council ordered that 'steps be taken to purchase the Canton, Ely and Leckwith Common'. It appears that negotiations between Mr W.G. Cartwright, described in the council minutes as lord of the manor of Cardiff, and the council were proceeding slowly as by 1883 little progress seems to have been made.

By 1885 notes on the Manors of Cardiff reported that, 'The Cartwrights conveyed to the Cardiff Corporation, Ely Common, Canton Common, Waungron, Ely Green and the wastes on Ely Road; otherwise known by the more modern names of Ely and Canton Commons. The corporation paid compensation to the commoners'. One year later, on 12 April 1886, it was reported that 'a portion of Ely Common has now been railed in to form Ely Park', although apparently problems were encountered as the head constable was told a year later to summon anyone cutting turf on the common.

A Government Public Health Act had stated that cities should create parks for the health of its citizens. The responsibility for the design of the park was given to the director of parks, William Wallace Pettigrew, and the borough engineer William Harpur. The common had to be drained and after some initial reluctance a two-foot deep lake was built at a cost of £4,000 and completed by the end of 1896.

The *Cardiff Times* states in reporting the official opening that, 'Canton was *en fête*; it was a red-letter day in that populous district. In times past Canton has been long suffering, for while the other districts of Cardiff have had open spaces provided for the delectation of the public, Canton has had to wait. Now however their turn has come'.

Over one hundred years later the park seems more popular than ever particularly with Ely families many of whom are probably unaware that they are enjoying themselves on the former Ely Moor and Ely Common.

In the book maps are included to assist in understanding the location of various buildings as well as the development and growth of the area. The histories of the parishes and many of its industries were covered in depth in volume one so are not repeated in this book. There have been many requests from local residents to cover the period after the Second World War and it is hoped to some extent that this has been addressed.

While noting that the most recent developments have been on the fringes of Ely, Caerau and Michaelston-super-Ely, 1999 witnessed the loss of one of Ely's most prominent and well-known landmarks, Ely Hospital: an institution that had dominated its rural surroundings from when first built in 1862 and which still commanded a major presence in Ely some 137 years later. This volume gives some prominence to the different phases and uses of the building that started life as Ely Industrial Training School. Despite the efforts of the authors who argued that the original building should be retained and restored to play a part in Ely's future, this unique local landmark has now been swept away. Sadly in all the official records consulted in researching the history of Ely Hospital, the 'voice' of those residents who lived most of their lives in the institution, are not recorded. This part of the book is dedicated to all those residents who lived in Ely Hospital and similar institutions and whose story has still to be told. Shortly before the text for this volume was completed news broke regarding the closure of the oldest existing industry in the Ely area; Ely Paper Mills.

The area around Culverhouse Cross has, in the last twenty years, experienced as much rapid change as that which took place before and after the Second World War in north Ely and Caerau. Culverhouse Cross is the last stop on our journey, echoing memories of a nearby and now closed Ely landmark which bore the name the 'First and Last Café': as the name implied it was the first café on your way into Ely and the last as you travelled out.

Nigel Billingham and Stephen K. Jones

Acknowledgements

We acknowledge again all those people mentioned in the first volume: *Ely, Caerau and Michaelston-super-Ely*, for the kind loan of photographs, many of which have been used in this book. We would like to particularly thank the following, who have assisted us with this volume: Glyn Bowen, Gary Brace, Irene Brace, Roger Brind, and the staff of Trelai Primary School, Mrs Britton, Cardiff County Council (Education, Leisure and Amenities Departments), Nora Coulson, Mrs Muriel Cumner, Paul Cumner, Beryl and Ray David, Rowena and Fred Davies, Barbara Dean, Owen Eardley, Mr and Mrs Edwards, Simon Smith and the staff of Ely Hospital, Peter Evans of Finning Ltd, Anne Gardner, Violet Gear, Gary Greenslade, Michael Hale, Sam Hutcheson, Barbara Jones, Douglas Jones, Ken and Doreen Jones, Charlie Morris, Marjorie Macdonald, Una McElveen, Laura Molan, Dennis Morgan, Mrs Newman, Mary Powell, Gill Reeves, Martin Roberts, Steve Rowson, Sian and Jude for their support, Dave Smith, Ken Smitham, Flt Lt F.E. Thomas RAFVR(T), Flying Officer Jeff Thomas RAFVR(T) and their colleagues at 30(F) Cardiff Squadron, Mrs Ann Tucker, Mr Alan Vaterlaws, Dr Stuart Owen Jones of the Welsh Industrial and Maritime Museum, Linda Williams and all the staff at Ely Library, Maria Wilkins, Brynmor Williams, Martyn Williams, Mark Williams, John Winslade and Gloria Yates, Whitbread Archive and the Wroughton History Group. Special thanks go also to Roy Denning, editor of *The Diary of William Thomas 1762 – 1795* which has been an invaluable reference guide for this and any study of the Ely area, and Jack Julian for access to his unpublished notes on the Ely Home Guard.

One

Ely Common
to Ely Bridge

The journey through Ely, Caerau and Michaelston-super-Ely begins at Victoria Park. It should be remembered that it is only since Wednesday 16 June 1897 that Ely Common became known as Victoria Park. The original intention was for the park to be called Ely Common Park and then Ely Park but, because the opening coincided with the celebrations marking Queen Victoria's Diamond Jubilee, the name was changed. Before the park was planned the area had been known for hundreds of years as Ely Moors. The records of the County Borough of Cardiff record the detail of an Exchequer special commission that took place in 1638 and stated: 'And that there are marsh lands in the county, adjacent to, the parishes of Landaffe and 'Leckwith in the same county called Leckwith More, Canton C[omon] and Ely Moore containing 200 acres. Each of the annual value of 2 pence and abutting the high road leading from Cardiff aforesaid towards Cowbridge on the north'.

The Llandaff Act books record the granting of leases to various people. For instance in 1673 a '...lease granted to William Mathew of Landaffe, of a house and 7 acres in Ely Moor and Gwaine Tullgoed for 21 years at 8s 4d'. Another example was a lease granted to 'Mary Davies spinster (daughter of Francis Davies, clerk, deceased) of 2a on Eley More, 1/2 a near Wain Wilt, 1a more in Eley More called Erw Wen, as also 7a called Anne's Pewterer's Lands'. In the 1780s it was ordered that 'posts be putt where necessary on the road on Ely Common'. This was presumably to assist the stagecoaches that had begun running across the common and through Ely on the way to Cowbridge. This seems to be the first time that the Ely Moor is referred to as a common.

Victoria Park showing the ornamental lake.

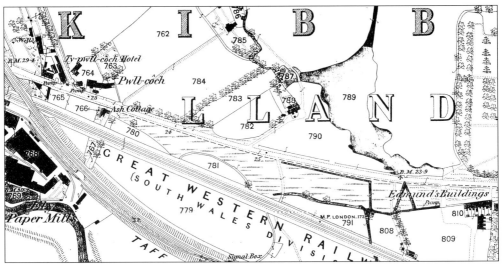

Ely Common, reproduced from the 1880 25in Ordnance Survey map. Ely Paper Mills can be seen on the left.

The Ely river, which burst its banks regularly up until its course was straightened in the 1940s. This flood, in November 1927, was in Victoria Park Road West and indicates the flooding Ely Moors was prone to. It is difficult to imagine now that, up to 1880, Ely Common was in the countryside and prone to frequent flooding when the River Ely burst its banks. The only real changes had been the building of the South Wales Railway, which opened in 1850 and Ely Paper Mills alongside the railway some fifteen years after.

Even in 1880 the last buildings in the area traditionally perceived as being Canton on the main road were the Clive Arms and Edmund's buildings. (The cottages still stand next to Pidgeon's the funeral directors.) The only other buildings were the Ty Pwll Coch hotel and farm with the Paper Mills on the other side of the railway before Ely Bridge was reached. However the laying out of the roads around the park was proceeding at a fast pace. On a conveyance map dated 1881 the area which became Victoria Avenue was earmarked to have two streets called Myrtle and Primrose Street. The map still delineated between land formerly 'Common land', 'glebe land' and that owned by Cardiff Corporation.

Victoria Park in 1927. All of the land in the photograph was originally Ely Common (Ely Moor). St Luke's church and hall stands in the middle foreground. In 1880 a paper mill worker arriving at the common described his journey to work, 'crossing the bleak common was an unpleasant ordeal, especially in bad weather. At night, more so, as there were no lamps then, or proper footpaths. It was a case of up and down – jumping the channels made to drain water off the roads. Victoria Park was a wild barren waste common with a pond in the centre. It was common land to which the people had a right, and everyone around who owned quadrupeds of any sort turned them out and it was a great boon. Being near the town, it was never free of gypsy caravans'. Lansdowne Road was extended to the park in the early 1930s. On 21 and 22 June 1997 the park celebrated its centenary with the unveiling of a statue of Billy the Seal. Sunday 6 September 1998 saw the opening of a new bandstand. The original bandstand had fallen into disrepair after the Second World War and was demolished in 1954.

A summer evening return excursion from Barry Island to the Rhondda passes Ely Paper Mills signal box on a Saturday evening in July 1963.

Ely Paper Mills signal box, 1951. Beyond the signal box built by Taff Vale Railway, can be seen the main South Wales to London line and the backs of houses in Cowbridge Road East.

Ely Paper Mills level crossing with Ash Cottage (left) on 17 March 1931. The crossing, which was opposite Mayfield Avenue, allowed pedestrians and traffic access to the paper mills. However, by 1932, Sanatorium Road and Paper Mill Road had been built and the crossing was no longer needed for vehicles.

A Castle Class 4-6-0 on an up Swansea–Cardiff train passing the post office sorting office on Cowbridge Road East. The upper section and roof of the Ty Pwll Coch is visible behind the building. The sorting office occupied the site of the former Thomas Owen Ely Paper Works Institute building. The Institute building fell into disuse after a fire following which the Paper Mill Welfare Association purchased the sports field in Mill Road, Ely.

The same level crossing a year later on 31 March 1932. This view shows the footbridge shortly before completion.

Ely Paper Mills showing both the level crossing and the Institute building (middle background), in 1922.

An aerial view of Ely Paper Mills looking towards Llandaff taken on 21 September 1948. The Ely river is in the foreground showing its new course along with Ely farm (bottom left).

Ely Paper
Works headed
notepaper
dated 16 April
1923.

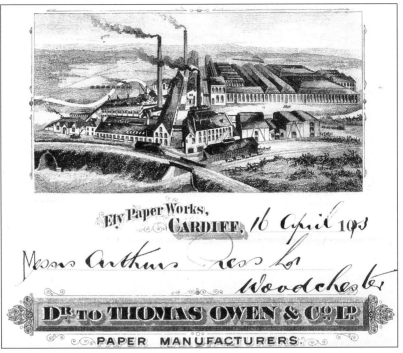

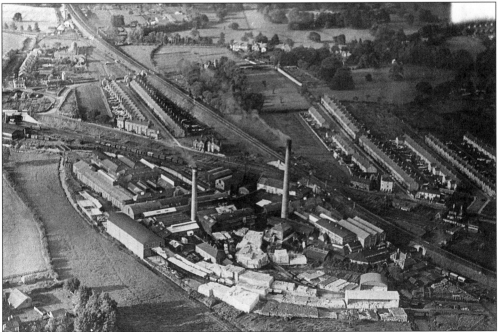

Ely Paper Mills, 1923. This photograph shows the rural surroundings before Western Avenue was built in the mid-1930s. The River Ely winds its way through the paper mill buildings with Ely farm in the left foreground. The Taff Vale Railway runs across the view diagonally, with Aldsworth Road running parallel. The Ely roundabout is middle left with the Railway Hotel behind. The level crossing before its alterations can be seen middle right with Windway Road, Mayfield and Fairfield Avenues half completed.

Ely Paper Mills and old Ely, 11 October 1968. The crossing over of the two railway lines assists as a reference point on the two photographs.

Ely Paper Mills (Thomas Owen) baseball team, 1958.

Ely Paper Mills (Thomas Owen) cricket team in the 1930s.

Ely Paper Mills siding showing mixed gauge railway turntable, 15 June 1932. A relic from the broad gauge days of the first railway to pass through Ely, the South Wales Railway, this turntable was still being used for standard gauge wagons in 1932. Opened in sections (the first section being Chepstow to Swansea on the 18 June 1850) the SWR was to form part of the Great Western Railway empire. Engineered by Isambard Kingdom Brunel the line was built to the 7ft (broad) gauge adopted by the GWR. In South Wales the broad gauge was converted to standard gauge in 1872 so the turntable must have been in use before that date. By 1932 the turntable was only in use for standard gauge i.e. middle and right outer rails, which would have required considerable effort to turn with a wagon as it would have been 'out of balance' on the turntable. The type of rails used on the turntable are 'Barlow' rails laid originally on the west Wales section of the SWR. It is believed that the private branch line making up the siding and the turntable were simply concreted over when the mill switched from rail to road traffic.

A trolleybus approaching Ely Bridge in the late 1960s. By April 1968 Ely was the only part of the city to still have trolleybuses – services 10a/10b. When cracks were found in Ely Bridge on the 1 April 1969 its four lanes were reduced to two and Bailey bridges had to be temporarily built (see p. 29). Trolleybuses continued to use the old bridge until the third Bailey bridge was complete. By October 1969 new Daimler Fleetline buses began running alongside the trolleybuses. The 11 January 1970 was to be the last date for a trolleybus to run on a normal service but due to a dispute at Roath the service unexpectedly ended on Wednesday 3 December. Despite this a 'Last Trolleybus Week' went ahead as scheduled with the system finally closing as planned on the 11 December 1969.

An early photograph of Loughers factory in Norbury Road. It was built about 1912 and specialized in bacon and jams. Two of their advertisements offered 'mild home cured bacon, hams, lard' and in the 1930s 'Llandaff and Ely valley jams'.

Alfred Lougher's stall in the covered market in Cardiff city centre. For many years Mr Lougher lived at 26 Ely Road, Llandaff.

The two breweries in Ely in the 1950s. Crosswells is in the foreground and the original Ely brewery to the rear right. Part of the Chivers factory is front right and Ely station is situated near the footbridge over the railway. The coalyard is located opposite the station and in the top left hand corner is Ely roundabout.

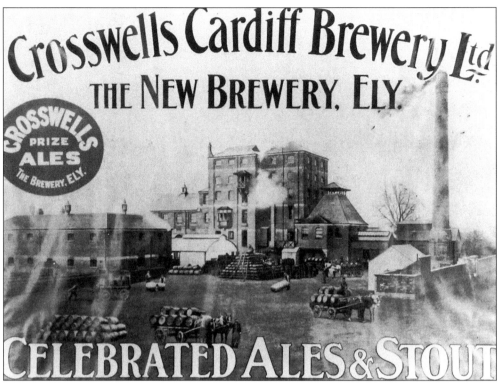

A Crosswells brewery advertisement in 1900, some three years after the brewery was built.

An Ely brewery outing in the 1930s.

An Ely brewery workers trip to Evesham, 1930s.

An Ely brewery three-ton Albion chain drive lorry in the 1930s. Many years before, in 1912, Mr Strong began his working life as a stable boy looking after five brewery horses. His job involved feeding the horses, attending to straw for bedding, and polishing the brasses – all before breakfast! He then accompanied a driver on delivery. He held the horses head while the driver went into the pub for lunch. Mr Winter was supplied with stone ginger while he waited.

Some of the female staff from Crosswells brewery, 1938. The brewery is in the background.

An Ely brewery outing in the 1950s. On the right can be seen the brewery offices, housed in the former Glyn Teg Hall.

A view of Whitbread brewery showing the footbridge over the railway in the 1950s.

The remaining employees at Whitbread brewery with the last Gold label beer bottled there in 1982, the year of the brewery's closure.

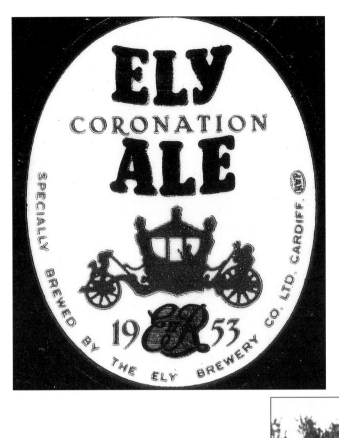

A label for Ely Coronation Ale which was sold in nip bottles at 1/6d in 1953. Ely was one of only two South Wales breweries to brew a special beer for this event. Other beers such as Brewers Own, Golden Gleam and Golden Harvest had been launched in the late 1940s. TV Ale, a new bottled beer sold in flagons at 2/6d was launched in October 1953. The idea behind TV Ale was to capture some of the drinking at home market following the introduction of television. This was followed by Strong Ale in 1954, Gold and Silver Stout in November 1957 and the new keg beer Silver Drum in 1958.

Samuel Chivers (1843-1918), the founder of the Chivers Pickle and Jam Factory, who was succeeded by his son, Ernest. The Chivers factory moved to Ely in 1900 and closed in 1980.

Two
Ely Bridge
to The Grand Avenue

Ely itself was a hamlet, part of the larger Llandaff parish. Samuel Lewis in his Topographical Dictionary of Wales *described the parish of Llandaff in 1834: 'LLANDAF…the parish is composed of five hamlets…[including]…Ely [containing] four hundred and seventy-four acres…at Ely Bridge, a populous village in this parish, additional fairs are held on July 22nd and December 11th…within the parish is a place of worship for Baptists, situated at the village of Ely'.*

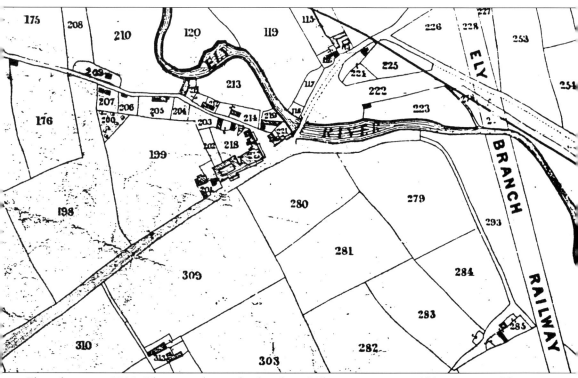

Ely tithe map, 1846. The map shows the hamlet of Ely as it was over 150 years ago. The proposed Ely Branch Railway of the Taff Vale Railway is shown with the main line (South Wales Railway) running across the top right hand corner. Ely Farm is situated bottom right. By the river bridge can be seen the old Bridge Inn and the nearby White Lion. The bottom left hand field (No. 310) is the site on which Ely Hospital was to be built.

The old Ely river bridge and the Bridge Inn/Hotel, around 1900. In 1881 Thomas Rees was the 'licensed victualler' as well as being a farmer of 5 acres. He was remembered by one Ely resident for his distinctive appearance: '…his mode of attire was typical of a "John Bull". His head adornment was a low crowned box hat with a broad rim, his coat a "swallow tail" which covered a light coloured waist coat with riding breeches and boots to match'.

Ely bridge in the 1950s. The buildings that are visible remain the same as fifty years previously (see above) although the bridge had, in the meantime, been rebuilt twice. In his diary for the 15 April 1768, William Thomas notes that: 'Mary Thomas alias Lewis, wife to William Lewis, innkeeper, of Eley Bridge' was buried. The penny reading craze was extremely popular in the 1860s and '70s with S.W. Allen stating in his reminiscences that: 'everyone took part in these functions and every large room that could be adapted was utilized…in Cardiff there was the Admiral Napier at Canton and the Bridge at Ely with the large barn of the farm close by'.

The widening of the railway bridge carrying Cowbridge Road in the 1930s. The view is looking towards the present day Ely roundabout. The railway bridge has been widened several times since it was built to carry the turnpike road over the South Wales Railway in 1850. The original stone arch is still in place (see p. 4) and is now in the centre of the roadway with the widened sections supported by steel girders, made by the Horsehay Company, Coalbrookdale.

This was the scene in the early morning rush hour on 3 April 1970, some three months after trolleybuses had stopped running to Ely.

The RAFA (Royal Air Force Association) club in Riverside Terrace with the branch committee and members. Setting up a branch of the Royal Air Force Association was first mooted on 30 October 1945. The Cardiff (Ely) branch, later Llandaff and Ely branch, of the RAFA held their first meeting at the Culverhouse Cross hotel, but this was felt to be out of the way for club membership. Subsequent meetings were held at the White Lion and it was here that the first general meeting was held in January 1946. After several years hard work, branch No. 387 RAFA, opened its own club premises and the event was presided over by Air Commodore H.E. Forrow CB, CBE, Air Officer Commanding RAF St Athan, on Saturday 1 July 1950.

Mr Harry Lane, master baker, whose shop was at 1 Clarke Street in 1934. He is seen here with his delivery van that was pulled by his horse 'Tommy'. The business operated for thirty-five years between 1925 and 1960.

28	NAME IN FULL CHRISTIAN AND SURNAME	RE ADMITTED ORIGINAL ADMISSION NUMBER	EXACT DATE OF BIRTH			PARENT OR GUARDIAN NAME	ADDRESS
			Year	Month	Day		
28	Williams Lloyd	1	93	5	23	Richard	14 Cowbridge Road
"	Meredith James	2	92	4	2	Joseph	76 Aldsworth Road
"	Hunt Leslie	3	92	5	18	Charles	3 Fairwater Grove
"	Crook Arthur	4	92	9	5	John	12 Fairwater Road
"	Webb Arthur	5	92	3	16	George Prier (Uncle)	2 Fairwater Road
"	Edwards Ivor	6	92	7	13	Henry	Ferndale Road
"	Morse Albert	7	91	1	2	Albert	56 Aldsworth Road
"	John David	8	91	1	7	Jenkin	52 Mill Road
"	Thorne Charles	9	89	7	16	William	15 Windsor Terrace
"	Fredrick Edward	10	90	8	4	John	10 Mill Road
"	Denning Leslie	11	93	8	3	James	13 Windsor Terrace
"	Denning Fred	12	91	7	17	James	13 Windsor Terrace
"	Lloyd John	13	91	2	2	John	14 Mill Road
"	Thorne Willie	14	91	10	17	William	15 Windsor Terrace
"	Prier Henry	15	92	9	4	Edwin	53 Aldsworth Rd
"	Davies Mary Myfanwy	16	90	9	11	Gwen	6 Bower's Row
"	Winter Rose	17	90	2	7	Thomas	Station Terrace
"	Smith Hannah	18	89	3	16	Harriet	33 Mill Road
"	Case Laura	19	88	7	26	Henry Davies	Caerau Cross Ways
"	Kingdon Jessie	20	89	4	29	Lucy	70 Aldsworth Road
"	Carry Hilda Mary	21	90	8	11	William Henry	6 Riverside Terrace

The first twenty-one children who were admitted on to the roll of Ely Council School (now Millbank Primary) which opened on 3 April 1902. Opened by the Llandaff School Board in Clarke Street, it can be seen standing opposite the only other building in the street at the time, St David's church hall. Shortly after opening, on 10 July 1902, the school also received the poorhouse children from the nearby Ely Industrial Training School.

Millbank School children in the playground on 16 July 1953.

A class photograph of Millbank School from 1965.

Bertie and Dennis Carson, the grandchildren of Sir Illtyd Thomas, at Ely Farm in 1923. These were the children of Sir Illtyd's daughter by his first wife, Mrs Holden Carson, who died in 1906. In 1926 he married for the second time, to Mrs Henrietta Morgan. Ely Farm, where Sir Illtyd was born, had been farmed by the Thomas family for three centuries.

Ely Farm in 1932. One of the first mentions of Ely Farm was the diary entry for 30 December 1764 by William Thomas. He states: '...was buried in Landaff Gwenlian (who lead a vile life with one William Jones, the fiddler, deceased for many years) daughter of the late Blanch of Ely Farm deceased. She was about sixty years of age'.

Ely Farm in 1932, one year after Mr and Mrs Davies moved to the farm.

Alderman Sir Illtyd Thomas, in 1907, the year he became Lord Mayor of Cardiff. Born on 6 June 1864, he was the son of George Thomas of Ely Farm and followed his father in the business of surveying and auctioneering. His municipal work started in 1895, becoming an alderman in 1905 and Lord Mayor two years later. His record of public service brought him a knighthood in 1925 and he was made an honorary Freeman of Cardiff in 1931. He died at his home, The Mead, Western Avenue, on 23 June 1943.

Marion Davies in the Orchid House of Windsor Market Gardens, sometime before it closed in about 1964.

The *Cardiff Times* recorded the opening of Ely Methodist church on 27 May 1911: '...The new church...occupies a prominent position on Cowbridge Road...it has been planned for use as a church and school pending the erection of a schoolroom on the adjoining land'. This photograph, taken in the 1960s, shows the 'schoolroom' at the rear, which had been acquired from Albany Road church in 1925 for £815. The 'temporary' building was finally demolished in the late 1970s and the church became a dual-purpose building. The church originally had an extra 16ft frontage to the main building but this was lost when, in 1924, the entrance steps had to be redesigned to accommodate the widening of Cowbridge Road by the Cardiff Corporation.

An Ely Methodist sisterhood outing outside the church in 1925.

Ely Methodist Sunday school on Whit Sunday 1 June 1952. The venue for the treat was the old

Ely Wesleyan Methodist Sunday school outing, around 1900. The 1874 date on the banner is a significant one in the life of the church's Sunday school. It was the year when a controversial meeting was held to discuss the problem of the continuing decline of the chapel's Welsh speaking membership. A decision was made to reform the Sunday school with English speaking class leaders under the superintendence of Daniel Williams who was the Ely stationmaster. Thirty pupils began at the school but this was to rise to seventy-five, only three years later. The Sunday school minute book makes interesting reading and records that a problem with 'truancy' obviously arose this year, as a rule was passed that scholars must attend not less than twenty-five Sundays in the year or be excluded from all treats connected with the school.

Ely racecourse and the backdrop is the stand built in the 1950s for sporting occasions.

Ely Methodist Band of Hope, Mill Road 1902. 'Queen Temperance' is Regina Rees and 'King Alcohol' is Captain Harris. Many revival meetings were held, although one such event was talked about for days – it was when George Brown was converted, shouted hallelujah and put 10s in the collection!

Bob Regan's outing, 1920. Mr Regan owned a shop at 4 Riverside Terrace (which was built in 1886). Nora Coulson (*née* Woolven) remembers moving there in 1909 when there was, '…one tap behind the back door and water had to be carried out to the lavatory. At the bottom of each garden was a stone stile which led to a well at the bottom of the terrace'.

Old cottages at Ely, 22 October 1888. The tithe map (see p. 27) shows these cottages on plot No. 219, situated just behind the Bridge Inn. This area constitutes the centre of the old Ely village. Residents from these cottages had to obtain domestic water from a well built into a garden wall opposite the old Wesleyan chapel in Mill Road.

Mrs Jane Sanders and her children, Olive, Kenneth, Thomas and Arthur, outside their house in Robert Street.

A 1930s advertisement for Treseder's nursery from *The Story of Llandaff Cathedral*. Stephen Treseder was recorded as living at Pwll Coch Farm, 538 Cowbridge Road (East) in 1889/90. An advertisement some seventeen years later gives the location of his nurseries as 'Pwll Coch and Ely'. In 1907 he claimed to be the largest rose grower in South Wales with his catalogue featuring a rose he had named after his wife and described as: '...colour pale lemon, deeper centre, opening to large full flower of good form and fine foliage'. He also claimed that his nursery was 'five minutes walk from Ely Station, GWR, and three from the Canton Tramway terminus'.

Telephone : 493 LLANDAFF

Telegrams : "CEDAR, CARDIFF"

STEPHEN TRESEDER & SON

ELY NURSERIES

540 Cowbridge Road

CARDIFF

Town Shop :

Principality Buildings - Cardiff

Two of Osmond's vehicles on Cowbridge Road (Windsor Terrace) around 1910. Jim Edwards is seen below standing in the centre, by his vehicle. The Osmond brothers were haulage contractors and operated the quarry at Culverhouse Cross. At one time the family lived in the Great House, which stood on the site of the Ely British Legion Club on Cowbridge Road (West). However, in 1915, William Osmond is listed as a contractor living at Springfield House, Caerau, with Thomas Osmond listed at 'Ingleford' on Cowbridge Road (West) which was situated opposite the Great House. They are also recorded as being based at Ely stables, which was located at the rear of 22 and 24 Cowbridge Road (West).

Regent Cinema, Mill Road, May/June 1984. The Regent opened in October 1928 and had 1,590 seats. It was described at its opening as follows: '...the interior decoration consisted of orange, pale green and black complemented with a screen boasting to be one of the largest in the Principality with costly electrically controlled curtains exquisitely designed and coloured'. Entry was priced at 6d, 9d or 1/3d and customers arriving by car in the mid-1930s could have their car parked for them. After the showing of the last film the building was, like so many former cinemas, converted to a bingo hall. The Regent fulfilled this role for twenty-five years – as the Top Rank Club seen here – with the old cinema lettering still legible on the walls. The Regent has now been demolished and a new development on the site, a care home to be known as Regency House, is nearing completion.

The cinema projectionist at the Regent.

They are now disused and falling into ruin. The Cardiff water works Compy. having brought up the whole.

Ely Mills, 21 October 1888. A mill had existed near the site of the mills in the sketch since 1126, when Bishop Urban was given the mills and adjoining land as a gift. In 1858 the corn mill still appeared to be flourishing and was in the ownership of Mr and Mrs Griffith David. However, by the time David Jones of Wallington made this sketch, the mills were uninhabited. The map shows Ely Mill at the end of what is known locally as 'Birdies Lane'. At this point there was a forded crossing of the river with a path going under the main railway line towards the hamlet of Fairwater. Built by the railway, the low headroom underbridge, or 'cattle creep', provided access for the farmer's animals and also accommodated the Fairwater Brook on its way to the river. Cardiff water works opened in 1852 and the first engineer was Alfred Gardener who arrived from Ware in Hertfordshire; his son later succeeded him as the engineer.

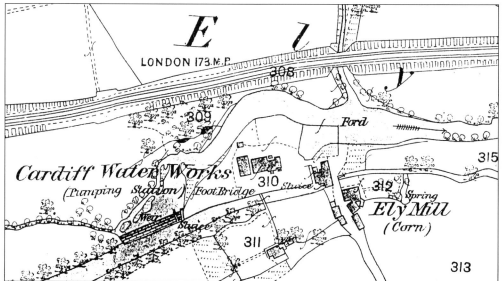

The location of Ely Mill and the Cardiff water works, reproduced from the 1880 25in Ordnance Survey map. Only the waterworks, in the form of a later building, remain today. The Fairwater Brook, flowing into the river under the railway, is now culverted. 'Birdies Lane' can be seen at the bottom right.

The racehorse 'Ely' with Mr Tom Olliver (trainer) and Will Johnson (stable lad) in 1865. 'Ely' was owned by Mr W. Cartwright, a large landowner in Ely and Llandaff, and the Lord of the Manor of Llandaff in the 1850s. (He gave his name to Cartwright Lane, although it is more popularly known as 'Birdies Lane'.) Cartwright was a keen racehorse owner and his horses were trained by Tom Olliver at his Wroughton stables in Wiltshire. In 1860 'Ely' was foaled and went on to win over nineteen races including the Ascot and Goodwood cups as well as races at Newmarket, York and Doncaster. Wroughton Place is a reminder of horse racing's glorious past in Ely, being named after the Wiltshire stables. In 1915 four of the buildings appear to be occupied in Wroughton Place along with the Chivers pickle and jam factory.

Mr and Mrs William Thorne and their daughter Sarah in 1905. The Thorne family owned the West End brickworks, which stood in Church Road, Caerau. Ten years later, the family were living in Windsor House on Cowbridge Road (West), next door to Osmond's the quarry owners.

Ely British Legion outing in the 1950s. The idea of setting up a club for ex-servicemen in Ely dates back to 1936. This was a time of depression with over 3,000 men unemployed in Ely alone; however an opportunity to purchase the White House on Cowbridge Road (West) was seen as too good to miss. In 1964 Mr George Piper described the state of the White House as they found it: 'The whole place was a shambles – the roof had great gaping holes, there was no lead piping and not even a floor that was sound. In fact the ragman had picked it over and there wasn't much left for us to work on'. Volunteers worked to repair the house and create a club and, as money was short, 'we even had to borrow the three guineas for the licence'. By the early 1960s a purpose-built club was being proposed which would cost £48,000. On the 12 February 1964 a new British Legion clubhouse was opened by Major T.J. Philpott, chairman of the British Legion in Wales.

Ely Conservative Club outing in the 1930s. Like the Ely British Legion above, the West End Club, the Home Guard Club and the Ely Consevative Club were based in what had been a private house (or rather two): Nos 24 and 26 Cowbridge Road (West).

Three
Around Ely Hospital and the Racecourse

The origins of Ely Hospital are that of an industrial school. In 1862 the Board of Guardians agreed to erect an industrial school, appointing a committee including Col. Tynte and Mr W.E. Williams of Redhouse Farm to take the project forward. Just over a month later the committee reported to the board that a suitable site had been found, surprisingly enough on Redhouse Farm land! Following this the clerk was requested to open negotiations with a view to purchasing the site from the estate of the Baroness Windsor.

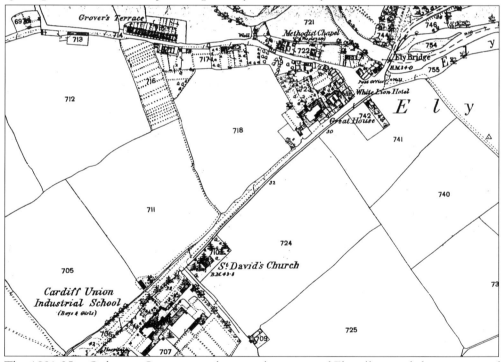

The 1881 25in Ordnance Survey map showing the extent of Ely village and the positions of Cardiff Union Industrial School (later Ely Hospital) and St David's church. The Great House, which was to become the Ely British Legion Club, is marked. As can be seen, there are only two houses on the south side of Cowbridge Road to the right of which is the present-day lane that runs through to Clarke Street. The post office is on the corner of Mill Road and Cowbridge Road with the first Wesleyan chapel situated further along Mill Road. The development of industry around Ely bridge (the Tower Brewery can be seen top right) saw speculative housing being built to house workers. Grover's Terrace, in Mill Road, being one of the first such developments (named after its developer I.B.K. Grover).

Left to right: Glynis Kiff, Stewart Hadley, Michael Sutton and Carol Blower outside St David's church in 1961. St David's church was built in 1871 to the designs of J.L. Pearson of London (who later designed Truro Cathedral) on a site donated by Lady Windsor. In 1897 the wooden pulpit was replaced with a stone pulpit found in Bonvilston churchyard. The chancel screen was installed in 1921 as a memorial to the men of Ely who died in the First World War.

The wedding of Mavis Thurston that took place at St David's church. The Thurstons were a Caerau family and the last residents of Church Farm, near St Mary's church, Caerau.

A painting, by an unknown artist, of Ely Industrial School in 1870. The buildings and the surrounding grounds of this establishment, known as Ely Hospital, have seen a number of developments (and uses) under the Poor Law Acts over the last 137 years including the industrial school, infirmaries and cottage homes. It is only in comparatively recent times that it has been associated with people with learning difficulties. (Reproduced courtesy of the Museum of Welsh Life)

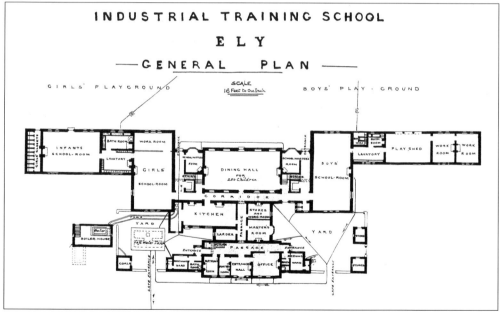

A ground floor plan of the Industrial Training School. In 1834 a locally controlled system of poor relief, overseen by central government, was implemented under the Poor Law Amendment Act. It was not, however, until 1861 that a 'separate establishment for children' was being considered as a necessary development of the Cardiff workhouse and it was then that the decision was taken to build this establishment in Ely. This series of plans appear to be the earliest existing general plans (not dated and possibly the original architects plans). A later extension to the dining room involved the removal of the first floor girls' dormitory (situated over the dining room). (Copyright Public Record Office)

Ely Hospital, 1914. Mrs Moore, the matron, can be seen with her dog. She appears as a slightly 'ghostly' figure caused by digital restoration of the damaged original photograph. The architect, Charles Edward Bernard, was chosen on the basis of the lowest tender and similarly David Jones of Penarth was chosen as contractor. The two storey, five window entrance block of the original building has been described as being in the Tudor Gothic style and carried the legend; 'Ely Industrial Training School 1862' inscribed in the stonework.

The Probationary Ward building, 10 September 1998. This was one of the new buildings erected at Ely as a result of Edwin Seward's report of 1894.

Ely Hospital staff outside the original Industrial Training School in the mid-1920s. The probationary block of the hospital can be seen on the left. Fourth from the left in the middle row is Mr Henry Harden Dean, deputy master, who worked at the hospital from the early 1920s to 1947, when he retired. He married Violet May Prowse, a nurse at Ely, in Llandaff Cathedral in 1930 and the reception was held at Ely Hospital, which was then known as Ely Lodge.

Work on the Industrial Training School began apace in August 1862 when a clerk of works (Mr Garrett) was appointed at 25 shillings a week and the work began in the autumn. The spring of 1863 saw the usual unforeseen additions and changes to the contract and in May a further £1,500 was applied for to pay for the 'architects commission, the cooking apparatus and fittings, laying on water, erecting a boundary wall and providing workshops'.

In 1875 the industrial school was described as a building accommodating '320 children who are educated and taught – the boys simple trades, the girls to make their own clothes and to undertake any position as servants. When they leave the school they are supplied with two new suits of clothes and other requisites but nothing that would in any way indicate they had been inmates in a workhouse'. The first intake of adult 'inmates' took place in 1898 and the opening of the first council school in Ely, in 1902, marked the end of the workhouse school. By 1915 the old school building had been altered and adapted for use as an auxiliary institution for adults. Some five years later the Cardiff Union Year Book stated that 'the auxiliary institution for adults was now occupied by lunatics, mental defectives and the infirm'.

49

Ely Hospital staff with Dr and Mrs Payne in the centre (seated) and Mr Hall, master of the children's homes, seated far left. In July 1935 Dr Payne reported that he had been medical officer for twenty-one years and it appears he took up his appointment at the children's homes after the Mental Deficiency Act 1913 became law. He reported at the time the difficulties of classifying patients and hoped for improvements if 16 acres of Ely Racecourse could be acquired. Dr Payne had made this point the previous year when arguing that the land was needed for patient segregation stating 'well educated and decent patients whose disability is solely due to senile changes…have to exercise…with idiots and imbeciles whose habits are distressing'. A nursing assistant who began work at Ely Hospital in the late 1940s reminisced about the patients working on the land but remembers that when it was wet they worked in the woodshed sawing up sleepers and sticks which were then sold. Other 'jobs' carried out by patients included pulling the truck that was full of meals round all the wards, scrubbing the passages, waxing and shining the floors, sweeping all round the hospital with one patient looked after the pigs. Visiting times were between 2 and 4 p.m. on Saturdays when 'patients were dressed in their best suits'. A bell rang to indicate the end of visiting time.

Ely Hospital staff group around 1940. The houses in the background are fronting Cowbridge Road (West). On the 5 July 1948 Ely was linked with Whitchurch Hospital to form Group 16 in the National Health Service, and was thereafter administered by the Whitchurch and Ely Hospital Management Committee. At this time Ely was designated a Mental Deficiency Institution and Mental Hospital. The first report under this management stated that Ely Hospital had 515 beds which were divided up as follows: persons of unsound mind: 243, mental defectives aged sixteen or over: 184, mental defectives under sixteen years of age: 54 and non-certified: 12. Of these patients, 318 had been resident for more than five years. In the NHS Plan for England and Wales, published in January 1962, it states that on the 31 December 1960 Ely Hospital has 200 beds for people with a mental illness. At the same time there was 424 beds for mental subnormality patients. The aim by 1975 was for there to be no beds for mental illness patients but the number of mental subnormality beds were expected to increase to 550. Under the heading; 'Care in the Community' the report stated that 'where illness or disability occurs, the aim will be to provide care at home and in the community for all who do not require the special type of diagnosis and treatment which only a hospital can provide'.

Despite the NHS plan, changes were to come about in a more dramatic way when, on 20 August 1967, Ely Hospital hit the headlines with a front page story in the *News Of The World* alleging various forms of misconduct. This was to culminate in the *1969 Report of the Committee of Inquiry Into Allegations of Ill Treatment of Patients, and other Irregularities at the Ely Hospital, Cardiff*.

A trolleybus on Cowbridge Road (West) around 1969. The building in the background is the small infirmary built in 1896 and extended in 1908, to serve the hospital. The infirmary building was to be the first casualty of the redevelopment of the site following the inquiry.

Ely cottage homes, 10 September 1998. These houses were completed in 1903 and consisted of an administration block containing the superintendents house and office, store, sewing rooms etc., two detached and two semi-detached houses with a room for a foster mother and twelve children (boys and girls) in each. A larger house had accommodation for a foster father and mother, relief mother and twenty-four boys. House No. 1 had accommodation for an assistant matron. The houses were built of 'red brick with Bath stone and Forest stone dressings with the intention that they should possess a brighter colour and consequently a more cheerful appearance than the adjoining buildings'. The homes, to be known as the 'Ely Headquarters Children's Homes', were occupied by the children on 2 May 1903. These buildings, like all the other pre-1969 buildings on the Ely Hospital site, have now been demolished.

The main building of the Cardiff (Ear, Nose and Throat) Hospital, 31 August 1981. The ENT had been originally built as an Isolation Hospital in 1907. On 3 January 1906 a deed of conveyance was signed by the Llandaff and Dinas Powis Rural District Council purchasing: 'five acres of land in the parish of Caerau for the Infectious Diseases Hospital'. On the same date a tender was accepted from David Davies of Trade Street for £9161 2s 5d to build the hospital. At the end of the month a clerk of the works was appointed at £32 15s per week. Eighteen months later the chairman of the council, Mr R. Forrest, formally opened the 'new Isolation Hospital at Ely' on the 15 August 1907. The matron was paid £50 per annum with a nurse receiving £26. George Williams of Ely was appointed as the lodgekeeper.

The waiting room of the Cardiff (ENT) Hospital after its refurbishment in April 1956. The Cardiff Ear Nose and Throat Hospital was treating 1,730 patients per year in 1969/70. There was fifty-six beds for in-patients; the cost per in-patient worked out at £56 9s 0d per week. The hospital was demolished in 1992 and currently awaits development as part of the Ely Hospital site.

'Blue Pencil' being led out onto Ely Racecourse in the 1930s. The races, as well as being an important event for the riders, owners and trainers, was also a big day for Ely residents. Nora Coulson remembers: 'we used to mind bikes in our fronts [Riverside Terrace] and you could tell who won by what they gave you, 6d, but more often than not 1d or 2d. We used to go by the hedge where the water jump was, had to be quiet when the horses came by and we were splashed with water. After the races we used to go through the hedge into the racecourse, up into the stands to see what we could find and we had money, empty bottles, cigarette cards and sometimes coats'.

The start of the Welsh Grand National on 10 April 1912. The inset (right) shows a portrait of Mr C.B. Ismay's winning horse 'Jacobus', ridden by F. Lyall.

Ely racecourse grandstand with William J. Tatem, 1st Baron Glanely of St Fagans (1868-1942). A prominent Cardiff ship owner who lived at The Court, St Fagans (see p. 105-7 and 119), he took up horse racing in 1909. He owned stables near his other home, 'Exning' at Newmarket, where all his horses were trained after the First World War. W.J. Tatem was knighted in 1916 and created 1st Baron Glanely of St Fagans in recognition of his contribution to the war effort. He won the Derby in 1918 with 'Grand Parade' (horses from his stable would win all five classic races). The following year Lord Glanely broke the record for the price of a yearling receiving 11,500 guineas for 'Westward Ho'. In 1929 he was elected to the Jockey Club and the following year his horses won both the Oaks and St Leger (the latter won on his horse 'Singapore').

Sheep dog trial programme from 1895. These were a regular event on the racecourse at the turn of the century.

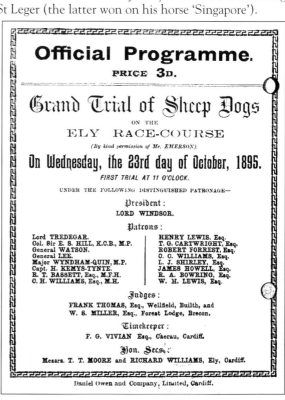

Official Programme.
PRICE 3D.

Grand Trial of Sheep Dogs
ON THE
ELY RACE-COURSE
(By kind permission of Mr. EMERSON).

On Wednesday, the 23rd day of October, 1895.
FIRST TRIAL AT 11 O'CLOCK.

UNDER THE FOLLOWING DISTINGUISHED PATRONAGE—

President :
LORD WINDSOR.

Patrons :

Lord TREDEGAR.	HENRY LEWIS, Esq.
Col. Sir E. S. HILL, K.C.B., M.P.	T. G. CARTWRIGHT, Esq.
General WATSON.	ROBERT FORREST, Esq.
General LEE.	O. C. WILLIAMS, Esq.
Major WYNDHAM-QUIN, M.P.	L. J. SHIRLEY, Esq.
Capt. H. KEMYS-TYNTE.	JAMES HOWELL, Esq.
R. T. BASSETT, Esq., M.F.H.	R. A. BOWRING, Esq.
O. H. WILLIAMS, Esq., M.H.	W. H. LEWIS, Esq.

Judges :
FRANK THOMAS, Esq., Wellfield, Builth, and
W. S. MILLER, Esq., Forest Lodge, Brecon.

Timekeeper :
F. G. VIVIAN Esq., Caerau, Cardiff.

Hon. Secs. :
Messrs. T. T. MOORE and RICHARD WILLIAMS, Ely, Cardiff.

Daniel Owen and Company, Limited, Cardiff.

The crowning of the May Queen on Ely Racecourse in 1932. This was an annual event organized by the Congregational church (Later Ely URC); the event also included maypole dancing.

Excavation hut on Ely racecourse, 1894. In the spring of 1894 John Storrie persuaded the Cardiff Naturalists Society to support archaeological excavations under his superintendence on the racecourse. He believed that the mounds there covered ancient remains and, having obtained permission from the landowner the Rt Hon. Lord Windsor, work began on the 30 May 1894. The tenant was George Thomas of Ely Farm, who told John Storrie that the mounds stood in what had been known as the 'Monachlog' and which he and older inhabitants believed was a monastery site! An exploratory trench revealed evidence of Roman buildings on the site, but digging ceased on the 22 August 1894 when funds ran out. Some of the finds, in the form of pottery fragments, coins and other small items, were presented to the Cardiff Museum and the diggings filled in. In 1922 R.E.M. Wheeler (later to become famous as Sir Mortimer Wheeler) returned to the site, obtaining consent from the then landlord Lord Plymouth (the tenant being William Emerson) to resume excavations. While acknowledging Storrie's role in identifying the site, Wheeler was critical of his conclusions. He was, however, in general agreement that it was a Romano-British residence dating back to the first half of the second century and that iron working had been carried out on site.

Ely Rovers whose home ground was Ely Racecourse. Formed in the 1933/4 season, their junior team went on to win the Cardiff & District League on three occasions.

Ely United AFC winners of the Welsh Sports Club season 1926/7. The photograph was taken against the background of the racecourse stand.

FOR ONE WEEK ONLY.

mperial Airways AIR LINER " Prince Henry"

t ELY RACECOURSE, MONDAY, April 27,

Till SUNDAY, May 3 (inclusive).

LYING NOON TILL DUSK.————————SUNDAY 10 a.m. TILL DUSK.

Passenger Flights 10/6, 7/6, 5/-.   Special Flights in Avro 10/-.

ALKING THE WINGS IN MID-AIR, to be followed by ARACHUTE DESCENTS at 6.30 p.m. (weather permitting)

On WEDNESDAY, SATURDAY, & SUNDAY.

Admission 6d. Children 3d. Car Park 1/-.

An advert for Imperial Airways Airliner at Ely Racecourse, 29 April 1931. Beryl David (*née* Jones), of Ty Coch Road remembers her mother going up on one of the 5 shilling flights – 'although it was a great thrill it was a considerable sum of money for those days'.

CARDIFF RACES AND STEEPLE-
CHASES
Will take place
ON WEDNESDAY AND THURSDAY,
28TH AND 29TH APRIL, 1886,
Over the well-known Ely Race Course.
SIX RACES EACH DAY.
Large entries both days.
FIRST DAY.
In place of the race that did not fill
THE ELY HUNTERS' HURDLE RACE
Of 25 sovereigns, for hunters the property of residents
in the Counties of Monmouth and Glamorgan, that
have been fairly hunted with any established pack
of hounds in these counties through seasons 1885-86 :
4 years old, 11 st. ; 5 years, 11 st. 10 lbs. ; 6 years and
aged, 12 st.   A winner once 7 lbs., twice or oftener,
14 lbs. extra.   Entrance, £1 ; no restriction as to
riders.
Two miles, over eight flights of hurdles.   To close to
the Clerks of the Course at the Royal Hotel, Cardiff,
by seven o'clock the evening before running.
Messrs WAIN and GOTTWALTZ, Hon. Secs.   78808

ROATH HALL, CARDIFF.—Messrs
JOHNSON and ROBERTS' Annual Ball will
take place on Easter Tuesday, 27th inst. Tickets to
be obtained of Messrs Heath and Sons, Crockherb-
town, Cardiff ; or of Mr F. G. Roberts, Mozart House,
Roath. Ladies, 4s ; Gentlemen, 5s ; Double Ticket,
8s 6d.   79251

An advertisement for Cardiff races at Ely, 28 and 29 April 1886. This was a significant date in the history of racing at Ely. The *South Wales Daily News* reported that 'after an interval of eight years Cardiff was, on Wednesday, once more the scene of racing and judging from the amount of public interest taken in the proceedings there would appear to be good ground for believing that, if not for all time, at any rate for a long time to come, the inhabitants of the Welsh metropolis may look to the annual recurrence of the event'. It was in 1895 that the first Welsh Grand National took place at Ely.

Trelai football XI were Youth Division winners in the 1963/4 season. Left to right, back row: Paul Cumner, R. Thomas, K. Long, A. Foster, H. George, H. Williams. Front row: B. Waterfield, D. Pugh, F. Nicholls (captain), G. Palmer, L. Kear.

Trelai School girls' baseball team with Mrs Doreen Lane (*née* Fowler) in 1957. This was the first year for the girls' baseball team. The school magazine described the year: '…the girls under Miss Fowler's able direction, got off to an enthusiastic if shaky start…they scored their first convincing victory over Windsor Clive. Jeanette Payne and Pauline Morgan topped the scoring with 10 and 8 respectively…all in all this will be a side to be reckoned with in the future'.

Trelai Junior School football team at Millbank School, 1953/4. Back left are teachers Sid Merrifield and Joe Cross and back right is Ron Williams. The team's score sheet in this season read ten matches played, of which they won six, lost three and drew one. They scored thirty-five goals in total and their top scorer was John Davis, who scored fifteen. The school magazine said he had a memorable season, being the captain of Trelai, leading goal scorer and playing for Cardiff boys on six occasions.

Trelai Junior School staff. Left to right, back row: Andrea Smitham, Gwilym Roberts, Grace Stevens, Joe Cross, Joy Lloyd, Paul Kite, Janet Jenks, Garfield Jones. Front row: Joe Raybould, Jennifer Thomas, Ken Smitham, Barbara Groves, Merlyn Richards (head teacher), Des Jones, Rhian Caddy, Ken Phillips, Avril Geech.

The building of Trelai School extension in January 1961. The school first opened on the 4 September 1951 to educate the children of all the families on the new council estate in south Ely. One onlooker described the situation: '…350 children, many complete with children and other accessories, arrived en-masse at our portals. Three classrooms of the school were almost fit for habitation and workman swarmed over the rest. Three classrooms for 350 children meant declaring a holiday. Two days later canteen tables were brought into use meaning only one classroom was accommodating 80 children!' The onlooker continued: '…staff carried out expeditions to quaff tea and meet the headmaster…to offer him an aspirin'. Trelai School has only had three headteachers: Harold Morgan (1951-67), Merlyn Richards (1967-80) and Roger Brind (1980-present).

The Wheatsheaf Club after the fire on 4 March 1968. The club stood on part of the old racecourse where Bromley Drive has now been built. It was built as a sports and recreational club for the Co-operative Society.

A 1958 aerial view showing Highland Brickworks (right foreground) which opened at the turn of the century. The balloon barrage site with one of its large hangars can be seen (middle right). The wooded escarpment is now the line of the Ely Link road.

A closer aerial view of the brickworks showing Glyn Derw High School in the foreground. Alan Jones, a pupil at Trelai School, described his visit to the brickworks in 1963: '...first of all we saw a lorry tipping clay into a crusher and the clay being crushed into smaller and smaller pieces. The clay is steamed to get all the lime out and then cut by sharp wire. We saw the kilns and drying rooms. We also saw a new invention called a fork lift truck which can lift 500 bricks weighing two tons on to a lorry at one time'. At this time the brickworks were advertised as Welsh Brick Industries (1946) Ltd and stated they produced common bricks (pressed and wire cut) with high compressive strength.

Four
The Grand Avenue to Caerau Lane

The Grand Avenue, in the spirit of the Garden City Suburb developments, was designed to be the main feature of the new housing estate. Extending along its length are two main designs of semi-detached houses. The houses with bold round-headed porch arches appear to have been the favourite design among Ely restidents. These houses were known as 'Dutch' houses. Much of the housing stock was constructed by the firm of Bright and Addicott.

The corner of Heol-y-Felin and Mill Road showing one of the less successful house designs which were built using wooden and concrete sections. By the 1960s most of them were uninhabited and awaiting demolition.

William Thomas Morris and his wife Emma Beatrice outside Birlstone House, Cowbridge Road (West) around 1940. The Morris family were the first inhabitants of the house, which had been built by Bowles and Sons. In 1952 it became the surgery of Dr Gareth Davies and later became the home of Dr Geoff Morgan's practice until the surgery moved to Mill Road. The building, with the house next door, was refurbished and officially opened on 24 July 1991 as the Pendine Centre, a resource in the community for people experiencing mental health problems. The centre is run as a partnership between Cardiff Community Healthcare and Cardiff Social Services.

Marjorie King on her bicycle in Caerau Square in the late 1940s. Caerau Square was situated where St David's Crescent and Cymric Close now stand, although the houses were demolished in 1963.

Caerau Square in the early 1960s. A typical house had three bedrooms upstairs with a long hallway with a pantry, a sitting room and a large back kitchen downstairs. A toilet and a coalhouse were situated off the porchway. In an article the Revd Bolt remembered the end of Caerau Square after it had been evacuated: 'That eerie cobwebbed street, reminiscent of a ghost city left behind by a Klondike gold rush has now been mercifully removed. At its last it was a ghoulish row of skulls with empty eye sockets and toothless mouths agape.' (Published in the *Justice of the Peace and Local Government Review*)

Betty Wellerman with her daughter Gillian in Caerau Square in 1947.

The laying of the United Reformed church foundation stone (then Ely Congregational church) by the Lord Mayor of Cardiff W.B. Francis on the 7 September 1926. The notice in the press stated: 'The church is the first building of its kind to be erected in Ely on a site so generously given by the Cardiff Corporation'. The lease was for 999 years at 1/- a year. Following the ceremony tea was provided at Caerau Farm.

The 13th Cardiff (Saintwell) Guide Company, mid-1950s. The company was formed in about 1928/9, and was based at the old Saintwell chapel (see p. 121). Within six months Mary Powell, then aged seventeen, took charge on a temporary basis until a captain could be found. No captain was forthcoming so, by 31 October 1931, Miss Powell had progressed to captain herself, a post she held almost continually for forty-eight years. On 4 October 1932 the company moved to Windsor Clive School where it convened for nine years until Revd Glanmor Jenkins invited them to be based at the Grand Avenue Congregational church. Its first ever camp was at Merthyr Mawr in 1934, which cost about £10 for the week.

The Ely United Reformed church hall before and (below) after the fire on 18 December 1987. It became obvious in the 1930s that the dual-purpose church building could not cater for all the church activities and so in 1942 a determined effort was to raise money for another building. During the second half of the war, as emergency restrictions eased, a series of toy bazaars were held, bringing financial success and boosting the building fund. Toys were almost unobtainable, so the church members made all sorts of toys. On the 4 May 1947 a special church meeting was called to discuss a newspaper advertisement which offered: 'Dance hall for sale in Dowlais for £500'. The hall was purchased, dismantled, transported to Ely and re-erected at a cost of about £1,600 plus the purchase price. The hall was opened and dedicated on the 18 February 1948. Following the fire the church agreed to the hall site being used for the new building housing the Barnardo Family Centre and Cardiff County Council Social Services.

The 4th Cardiff Company of the Boys Brigade passing the Grand Avenue shops in 1946. The trees on Charteris Green have obviously been recently planted. The company began on 18 September 1931 under the captaincy of Mr Whitelock. Immediately after the war years the company had five meetings a week due to the number of boys wishing to attend.

The Revd Glanmor Jenkins with members of the Boys Brigade painting the railings outside the church on Grand Avenue in 1933.

The Revd Mary Evans (left) on the occasion of the Grand Avenue URC church 50th anniversary in 1977. Revd Mary Evans came to Ely, in 1966, to take up the post of minister at the Grand Avenue Congregational church, Grand Avenue and the place became the focus of her life until her retirement. As well as her direct work in the church and the Ely Council of Churches she involved herself in a whole range of community activities including play schemes, Ely Festival, a luncheon club for the elderly, Citizens Advice Bureau, Citizens Advocacy and for over thirty years church chaplain to Ely Hospital.

Mary was born into a non-conformist family at Village Farm, Bonvilston, and helped run the farm until she was thirty-four, when she trained for the ministry in Liverpool. Her first post was at Wooton-under-Edge before coming to Ely. Mary died suddenly on 13 June 1997 just a few weeks before she planned to celebrate forty years in the ministry. A service was held to celebrate her life on 13 July at the Church of the Resurrection and as the order of service stated: 'we give thanks for Mary – for her vision of the new earth through her pastoral care, counselling, support and friendship given to so many in Ely'. Along with the Revd Bob Morgan, Mary launched the first Ely book in December 1996 at Trelai Library (see p. 8).

The 15th Company of the Boys Brigade at the rear of Captain A.J. Harris's garden, 46 St Fagans Road, Fairwater, in 1909, the year the company started. There were four officers and forty boys at the outset and the company was in existence for twenty-five years before disbanding in 1934.

The Revd Glanmor Jenkins with the Cardiff 4th Company outside Grand Avenue Congregational church in 1937. The company won the South Wales and Cardiff Ambulance Cup (First Aid) and the Cardiff Battalion Ambulance Shield which are on show here.

The Cardiff 4th Company outside Grand Avenue Congregational church at the end of the war.

The wedding of Peggy Roberts and Archie Kellard in 1939. This was taken in Charteris Crescent following the wedding which took place in Grand Avenue Congregational church.

Alma Cridland and her mother outside their home in Red House Road in 1935. The road was named after Red House Farm which stood nearby and had remained a working farm until the farmhouse and its land was sold after the First World War to build the first phase of the Ely housing estate. It then became a construction yard and maintenance depot behind public buildings in Red House Crescent. It was officially known as 'Corporation PWD Red House Depot (Property Repair Section)'. The public buildings housed the Red House Clinic (Public Health) and National Assistance Board (later Ministry of Social Security). Part of the farmhouse was still used as a residence in 1958.

The 1937 Coronation celebrations in Red House Road.

The laying of the foundation stone for Herbert Thompson School in Plymouth Wood Road which was carried out by Mrs H.M. Thompson on 6 July 1925. The school cost £43,833 15s 3d to build.

The foundation stone ceremony for Herbert Thompson School, 1925. The school was named after Herbert M. Thompson, chairman of the Cardiff Education Committee and Vice-President of the University of South Wales and Monmouthshire. The site of the school was described as follows: '...on the north side of the Green Farm housing estate on sloping ground in an open and elevated position, where a canopied platform decorated with flags and bunting had been erected. The buildings will provide accommodation to 1,188 scholars. There will be 396 in each of the boys', girls' and infants' departments with domestic science and manual instruction in a separate block, and adequate play sheds (capable of conversion into open-air classrooms) with playgrounds and a playing field over an acre in area'.

Herbert Thompson Girls' School class in 1933. As previously mentioned the school was split, for older pupils, into girls and boys schools. The school was officially opened less than two years after the foundation stone ceremony on 2 May 1927. The school had been built at the point where the old Mill Road petered out near Birdies Lane and from where a track led to Red House Farm. Here two footpaths led to Cowbridge Road (West), one emerging at the junction of Cowbridge Road and Grand Avenue and the other by Crossways Road where Highmead House stood.

The staff at Herbert Thompson Girls' School in the early 1930s.

Herbert Thompson Boys' School class around 1936. Clifford Russ, who lived at 48 Charteris Crescent, is third from the left at the back while in the front row, fourth from the right, is Melvyn James Jones with his brother Lawrence Douglas Jones immediately behind.

Class 8 at Herbert Thompson School, 1931. Behind Herbert Thompson School and the adjoining Mill Road Recreation Park, are two old cottages (accessed from Birdies Lane) which are used today as a workshop and timber yard.

A Castle class engine heads up a London train near Birdies Lane looking in the direction of Wroughton Place and Crosswells brewery in 1961. The building seen on the right had originally been built as a furniture factory and was latterly occupied by Radius CBS. The site has now been developed for housing.

Ely Welfare Football Club outside Pethybridge Welfare Hall in the 1933/4 season.

Mrs Morris walking her alsatian dog in Plymouth Great Wood (commonly known as Plymouth Woods) in 1949. The photograph is looking in the direction of St Fagans. Covering 37 acres the wood is situated between north Ely and the railway line near St Fagans. The semi-ancient woodland contains over thirty different species of trees, many of which were planted by William Treseder on behalf of the Earl of Plymouth. On 14 August 1922 the wood was given by the Earl of Plymouth to Cardiff City Council and the donation was announced by Councillor R.G.H. Snook before he formally opened the open-air swimming pool at Splott (he is remembered today in Ely by the street name; Hill Snook Road). Cllr Snook stated: 'The Great Wood ought to be an ideal spot for picnic parties and would be kept open as a lung at Ely'. After suffering years of neglect a group called the Friends of Plymouth Great Wood was formed and, with the co-operation of the City's Sports and Leisure Department, the woodland now serves as an important local amenity with new footpaths, tree planting and a wetland area having been created.

Mr Charles Victor Brace celebrating the 1937 Coronation at 9 Frank Road by promoting his business as a 'Hygienic Electrical Service'. His shop was at 61 Clive Road in Canton although the family moved to Ely in the late 1920s. Mr Brace was born in 1892 in Worcester and served a five-year apprenticeship as a electrician, earning 2 shillings a week in the first year building up to 9 shillings before he qualified. One of his first jobs after arriving in Cardiff was as a projectionist at the Splott Cinema.

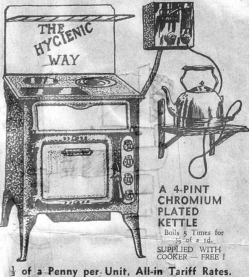
One of Mr Charles Brace's advertising leaflets from the 1930s. As the text states, Mr Brace was an electrical contractor to the City Council at a time when the north Ely estate was rapidly expanding and he was reassuring people that '…electric cooking is perfectly safe'.

The Melba Lounge (Milk Bar). This was situated at 105 Cowbridge Road (West) in the row of shops on the corner of Amroth Road. The photograph shows Charles L. Morris (right) with Mrs Emma Morris; Mr Elford is the customer on the left. The family owned two similar 'lounges' – one in Wilson Road and another in Penylan Road, Roath. In 1936 the post office occupied the corner of Amroth Road and Cowbridge Road (West), as it still does today, however, the end of the row was occupied by William David's grocery shop. The building housing Evans' fish and chip shop was not added until about two years later, closing off the old lane known as 'Hancocks Lane'.

Irene Hancock on the swing in the grounds of Hancock's Market Garden which was on land through which Amroth Road was to be built and south of Cowbridge Road. Hancock's detached house, now known as Highmead Villa, still stands on Cowbridge Road (West). Hancock's moved to Ely around the turn of the century when the area was open countryside. One of the Llandaff and Dinas Powis Rural District Council's minutes of 29 April 1908 conjures up a rural scene. It was agreed that 'a plank bridge be constructed to carry the footpath which leads from Britway Terrace, Ely to Caerau village across the stream in Mr Hancock's garden'. Before the building of Amroth Road 'Hancocks Lane' provided the main access to fields and buildings south of Cowbridge Road, running along the boundary of the Isolation Hospital. On 22 July 1931 'Hancock's field was purchased by the City Council from Mrs Yolland' to build the first council house development in south Ely.

Kilgetty Close Coronation street party in June 1953.

The opening ceremony of the Salvation Army Hall in Aberthaw Road on the 29 September 1939. The hall was built on land that had formerly been the grounds of Highmead House. Reminders of the house remain in the nearby street names, such as Highmead Road and Vachell Road (the name of the family associated with the house since the 1850s).

'Signet Ring', a whippet owned by Mr Fred Winter, which won the Gresford Colliery Disaster Fund Handicap Race. The race was backed by the Highmead Social Club to raise funds for the dependants of the 265 male victims of the disaster who were killed in an explosion at Gresford in Denbighshire.

Fred Winter with 'Signet Ring'. Whippet racing took place every Saturday afternoon in the field behind Highmead House. The 125-yard course was divided into six lanes by upright poles and ropes. The poles were placed at equal distances so that the dogs were not frightened when passing at speed. There was no printed card unless the race was a large handicap which were usually being held on a bank holiday. Races were organized as a sweepstake by the local race club and proceeds often went to charity. Bookmakers did attend but stakes were small. Dogs were handicapped according to recent performances and, to encourage them to run, 'flagging' took place (the waving of a meat cloth in front of them).

Five

Around Caerau

'CAERRA (CAERAU), a parish, in the union of Cardiff, hundred of Kibbor, county of Glamorgan, South Wales, 3 ½ miles (w.) from Cardiff, containing seventy-seven inhabitants'. This parish, part of which was given by Fitz-Hamon to Sir John Fleming, one of the Norman knights who attended him in the conquest of Wales, constitutes a prebend in the cathedral church of Llandaff, valued in the king's books at £3 10s 7_d. The bequest endowed Sir John with the tithes not only of this parish, but also of the parishes of Penterry and Llandogo, in the county of Monmouth. The 'living' is a perpetual curacy, endowed with £1,000 royal bounty, net income of £60, patron and impropriator, Prebendary of Caerau. The church, dedicated to St Mary, is chiefly remarkable for its situation within the precincts of a Roman camp, which is one of the most extensive and entire in the Principality. Its form is that of a regular parallelogram, rounded at the angles, and enclosing an area of about 12 acres. It is defended on the north side, where the ascent is steep, by one single rampart, on the south and south-west by two, and on the east side, where was the praetorium, by three ramparts. The praetorium, which is still visible, is of a circular form, guarded by a steep rampart, and is connected with the camp by a very narrow passage. ... The total expenditure of the parochial rates, for the year ending 25 March 1837, amounted to £52, of which £30 was for the relief of the poor, £7 towards county rates, and £15 for incidental charges. (From Samuel Lewis, Topographical Dictionary of Wales) (Note: Samuel Lewis is incorrect in his description of St Mary's as being situated within a Roman camp as it is in fact an iron age hill fort constructed by the ancient tribes of the area.)

Balloon barrage depot in the 1960s. Occupying a site previously used for growing vegetables under the control of the Public Assistance Committee of Cardiff City Council, RAF Llandaff (as the establishment was officially known) was to be brought into service by August 1939. There had been some protest by Ely councillors about the sale to the Air Ministry. They argued that Ely was a most unsatisfactory spot on which to build a balloon barrage depot, because in the event of hostilities this would naturally become a target for enemy aircraft and one would have thought they would have consideration for the hospital nearby. Mr George Williams, replying to this, said that he did not think a balloon barrage site was an attraction to the enemy, it was place they would try to avoid.

Officers and other ranks at RAF Llandaff, 1942.

A wing inspection at 30(F) Cardiff Squadron Air Training Corps (ATC), 1968. The ATC have been based in Ely since the early years of the Second World War. It was formed in 1938 as the Air Defence Cadet Training Corps and paraded on Sunday mornings at Cecil Street, Broadway, under the command of Sqdn Ldr Evan L. Roberts. In 1940 government recognition led to the forming of the Air Training Corp with the motto 'Venture Adventure'. The letter 'F' in the Squadron's title indicates they were one of the fifty founder members of the Corps and remains the only Welsh Squadron with this distinction. The squadron moved to RAF Llandaff (where the Western Leisure Centre now stands) and trained fourteen to eighteen-year-old cadets in signals, drill, principles of flight etc. before they joined the RAF as signallers and radio operators in Lancaster bombers. Cadets had to pay for their own uniforms, nicknamed 'Hairy Marys', at a total cost of £1 8s 10d.

March past in squadron review order, 30(F) Cardiff Squadron Air Training Corps, 1968. In 1968 the squadron moved out from the military buildings which were being prepared for demolition and into a new adjacent building in Caldicot Road known as No. 1 Welsh Wing Headquarters. The old hangar door runners can still be seen on the site and the shooting range is the only remaining building from the old war time station. In 1980 girls were allowed into the corps and today the squadron has a female commanding officer. The 60th anniversary of the squadron took place in 1998 and, in those 60 years, over 2,000 cadets have passed through training with the squadron achieving numerous sporting achievements and maintaining a link with the former airforce association with Ely.

The parade ground and buildings at RAF Llandaff in the 1960s. The rooftops of houses in Caerau Lane can be seen on the right.

RAF personnel during the Second World War. RAF Llandaff had been designed to accommodate twenty-four balloons in the defence of Cardiff but Lord Haw-Haw, in one of his infamous broadcasts, claimed that only seven had been allocated. Teams of ten men or sixteen women were required to handle the balloons which sometimes ran amok; 'In the first winter of the war…one of the balloons broke free of its moorings and created a trail of destruction along a Cardiff street. News of the rogue monster was hastily transmitted from Balloon Command's headquarters at Ely…from there a fighter plane was summoned to shoot it down' (From *Cardiff: A City at War*)

A view inside the Western Welsh depot, early 1931.

Western Welsh football team, 1933/34 season.

The choirs at the Ely Opera in 1984. The Ely Opera performed in the closed down depot of Western Welsh in Caerau Lane on two evenings in 1984 as part of the Ely Festival. There were about 500 in the audience each evening and 200 performers from Ely schools and the local community. The story was based on a semi-fictional Ely character from the nineteenth century called Thomas Jones. The project's final report summed up the cross section of people involved stating that '50 people danced in the final opera and their ages ranged from 8 to 70'. This was the last use made of the building before it was demolished. New development followed with the building of a Safeway supermarket on the site, the store now being operated by the German supermarket chain Lidl.

Caerau Lane seen through the window of a Western Welsh bus. The Western Welsh depot can be seen on the left with the timber huts of RAF Llandaff, later used by the Territorial Army and demolished to make way for the Western Leisure Centre site, on the right.

Caerau Park Crescent, 1944. Gareth and Roger Palmer with friend Ruth Ritter playing in their garden.

Caerau Lane Infants' School, 1952. Like Trelai School, Caerau Lane was built to accommodate the growing population of the new south Ely council estate.

A group outside Highfields public house, early 1960s. This photograph was possibly taken when the pub's Amateur Boxing Club was formed and some of the people included, from the Highfields ABC, are from the right, front row (kneeling): C. Britton, J. Hewlett, R. Condick, L. Lewis, P. Evans. Seated behind L. Lewis is E. Crowley (wearing glasses) who was the landlord of the Highfields and behind him is P. Rees. Standing in the centre of the photograph is J. Evans and the boxer Joe Erskine. The young boy standing in front of the pub porch is Billy Beatty.

An aerial photograph of St Mary's Hill and the racecourse, 1958. Clearly seen are St Mary's church and graveyard, the two brickworks and Ely Racecourse. Part of the racecourse has now been built over to create a council estate and Glyn Derw School. Heol Carnau can be seen in the middle with Heol Trelai behind.

A view from Cowbridge Road (West) towards Caerau Lane on 23 April 1963. Beyond the open space, now occupied by Caerau Court, can be seen the houses and maisonettes being built on Caerau Lane.

Caerau village, seen from St Mary's Hill, early 1980s. In the middle foreground is Ty Newydd farmhouse (next to the Hill Dip shop) with the Highfields public house behind. Beyond the Highfields can be seen Jacrow Square, a shopping centre (now demolished) built on land used as a car park by the Highfields. Richard Kay, a civil servant working for the Ministry of Defence, took the opportunity while travelling around Wales to visit and study archaeological and architectural remains. One of his notebooks (covering 1956-60) records his observations on Caerau: '…The village until a few years ago consisted of little more than a few [houses] on either side of the lane. This has now been lost in the streets of an extensive council house estate merging into the suburbs of Cardiff…'. (Photograph coutesy of Martin Roberts)

House building in progress at the racecourse end of Heol Trelai on the Trelai estate, 1947-9. Beyond the contractor's plant and fence can be seen the back of houses in Dew Crescent and Heol Eglwys with the chimneys of the paper mill in the background.

Officers and NCO's of 'B' Company, 11th Battalion, Glamorgan Home Guard on their 'stand down' in 1944. Their headquarters were in a disused garage and petrol station on Cowbridge Road (West) next to Mossford's monumental masons. Some of the soldiers are, back row, second left: Sgt Murrell and second from right: Lance Corporal Jack Julian. The Company Sergeant Major is the central figure in the middle row. Left to right, front row: -?-, -?-, Mr Brown, -?-, new CO, Dr Williams (MO), Mr Liddiard, Mr Murrell, Mr Prior.

Mr Jack Julian, who was a Lance Corporal in the Home Guard, wrote about their activities some years later: 'The Headquarters contained the company office, guardroom, armoury and stores. The spare land at the rear was just large enough for parades to assemble and fall in. In the cemetery wall opposite was a "pill box" or concrete strong point which covered the road up to Culverhouse Cross, including an anti-tank barricade position. This was situated about 50yds away where the road had specially strengthened points, lengths of steel girder could be fitted here into sockets to form an anti-tank barricade angled towards Culverhouse Cross. Michaelston Road, then a country lane, could also be blocked using a heavy tree trunk, festooned with barbed wire. It was pivoted at one end and supported at the end on an old wagon wheel. When needed it could be wheeled across the road and dropped into a specially deepened rut. The skittle alley of the Culverhouse Cross hotel was requisitioned as a miniature rifle (.22) range. During the later stages of the war, American forces stationed in the area occasionally challenged us to a shooting match there. The prize was usually a small barrel of beer. We never lost once…We also paraded at other venues as well. Some instructional parades were held at the Herbert Thompson School, though these were quite few. The other end of Cowbridge Road (West) was also defended, on the Paper Mill side of the road before crossing the railway, between the pavement and the embankment, was a concrete cylinder. This cylinder, now hidden by undergrowth, has a steel spigot on top providing a mounting for a "Blacker Bombard". This was the heaviest weapon that the Home Guard was issued with, capable of firing a 20lb projectile, that looked like a rugby ball with a stalk and fins, over 2,000 yards. The "Blacker Bombard" could only be fired once, and although we were trained in its use we never actually issued with one'.

The Home Guard at Saintwell around 1941.

Home Guard, No. 2 Platoon, in September 1942.

Left: St Mary's church, before restoration work in 1959. '...The old parish church stands on the crest of a hill to the south. A rough lane climbs steeply past a derelict brickworks and follows a little dingle to the summit of the hill. The church, a small edifice with a west saddleback roofed tower is by reasons of its elevations easily seen from a distance...'(from R E Kay's 1956-60 notebook). *Right:* The roofless shell of St Mary's.

The Revd John Guy moving the base of St Mary's churchyard cross during restoration work in 1961.

The first wedding to take place at the restored and rededicated St Mary's church on 22 August 1964. The couple getting married are Karen Paynter and Richard Brydon.

St Mary's, following restoration in 1960. A newspaper article from the early 1960s summarized the events: '…In both the eighteenth and nineteenth century the church underwent repair and restoration but following the building of St Timothy's in 1957 the church lay in ruins. Work commenced in 1959 led by Revd V.H. Jones who directed his band of helpers until the restoration was complete. In 1960 the vestry was added and after a great struggle the roof was replaced…while working on the nave floor Father Jones fell through into a previously undiscovered crypt. It was full of human bones, and although there was a staircase down it was completely blocked by these so the whole thing was sealed over and left undisturbed. Also the remains of medieval wall paintings were uncovered in the nave'. St Mary's was re-consecrated in 1961 by the Bishop of Llandaff who preached to a congregation which overflowed into marquees in a neighbouring field. Sadly by the early 1970s the church had been deconsecrated again and currently lies in ruins. Almost 300 years ago the church, which dates back to 1260, had ordered the casting of new bells for the church tower – will bells ever ring again in St Mary's church?'

Mr and Mrs Evan David of Penylan Farm, which dates back to at least the early 1700s. In that century tragedy struck the Lewis family who lived at the farm when four young children died from various diseases in a five-year period. Some ten years later the death of the children's father is recorded; he had killed himself through drinking.

Mr Niblett, the gardener at Caerau House, 1920. Mr Niblett lived at Church Cottage near St Mary's church cottage, which had long been derelict by the time Richard Kay described St Mary's Church in the late 1950s. 'It keeps company with the remains of a lone cottage and stands within an area of a most remarkable earthwork…' (from R E Kay's 1956-60 notebook). In a 1904 auction catalogue for the sale of the Caerau House estate the cottage was described as a '…gardeners cottage with a good garden surrounding, situated on the high ground, at the rear of the residence [i.e., Caerau House]. The property has considerable historical and antiquarian associations it being the site of a Roman Camp, and the old entrenchments are readily discernible'. The cottage and garden was three roods [one rood being a quarter of an acre] three perches [one perch being $5\frac{1}{2}$ yards] in size.'

Caerau Hospital staff, just before the hospital's closure in 1972. Left to right, standing: R. Arrowsmith, G. Hanson. Kath Prosser, F. Jones, Enid Hutcheson, Dr G. Thomas, K. Ellis, -?-, Muriel Cumner, Nora Dooley, M. Frayer, B. Scammell, Marjorie Paynter. Seated: an unknown wages clerk, Sister W. Thomas, Sister Price, G. Lockett. The history of Caerau Hospital lies in the need for Cardiff Council to provide a smallpox hospital. A loan was sanctioned to purchase Caerau House on 28 November 1923 but it was not until some four years later that the hospital opened. Over the years it opened and closed depending on the need for taking patients from as far away as Newport and Pontypridd. It also acted as an overfill unit for diphtheria and scarlet fever patients when (Ely) Isolation Hospital was full. After the war it housed chronically sick patients and in 1969 it was providing long term care for fifty-six patients. It finally closed in 1972 and has been a centre for homeless families ever since.

Muriel Cumner's daughter, Sian, outside her house in Heol-yr-Odyn around 1958. In the background can be seen the lodge for Caerau House.

The former mortuary building for Caerau Hospital, photographed by Martin Roberts shortly before its demolition to make way for new houses on Cwrt-yr-ala Road.

Left: The derelict barn of Sweldon Farm, 1979. The Emerson family had farmed there for generations and were the last occupiers of the nearby farmhouse. In the background can be seen Cyntwell High School. Following the establishment of comprehensive education in Ely based on Glyn Derw and Glan Ely, Cyntwell was allocated to Mostyn RC School (now part of St Mary Immaculate). *Right:* Caerau Crossroads, around 1939. Richard Kay (see p. 91) sketched this illustration of 'Caerau Crossroads' in his own time, while on official business. Sweldon Farm can be seen at the top of Sweldon Hill. (Reproduced courtesy National Monuments Records of Wales from the R.E. Kay Collection)

Whitsun treat for Mount Pleasant Forward Movement church (now the Ely Presbyterian Reformed church) at Ballas Farm, 1928/9. Farmer Watkins of Ballas Farm is in the middle row with the pipe.

Hancock's motor dray delivering to the Dusty Forge, 29 November 1955. Moorwell Motors supplied this Commer lorry new to the brewery and it became No. 48 in its delivery fleet.

Sweldon Youth Club netball team, 1951/2. Left to right, back row: Teresa Doonan, Carol Robinson, Mr Batchley, Teresa Millar, Audrey Clarke. Front row: Shirley Cunningham, Glenys James, Irene Burgess, Pauline Hill, Glenys ?.

Sweldon Youth Club baseball team, 1952/3. Left to right, back row: Mr Blatchley, Pat Cottle, Margaret Andrews, -?-, -?-, Pauline Hill, Mr Burgess. Front row: Dorothy Evans, Jean Cunningham, Shirley Cunningham, Irene Burgess, Teresa Millar, Brenda Dunscombe.

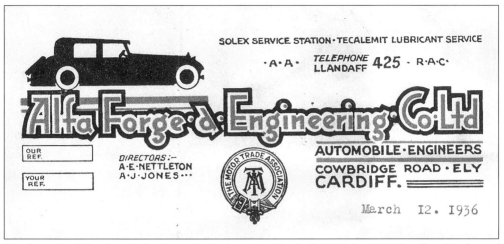

The letterhead for the Alpha Forge & Engineering Co. Ltd, 1936. In 1934 Geoffrey Tucker, of Deer Place, began his apprenticeship here at the age of fourteen. He left when he was eighteen and went to sea as an engineer.

The Alpha Forge Garage before 1939. The garage developed the trade started in the blacksmith's shop (which had expanded in the 1920s to serve the motor trade) from the Dusty Forge opposite. Arthur Nettleton was a director of the business along with A.J. Jones.

An artist's sketch of the new Bearings factory in 1948. This business, which bears the name of Bearings (Cardiff) Ltd today, has been a prominent engineering concern on the Cowbridge Road (West) for some sixty-five years. The business was started in 1934 from modest premises at the rear of the adjacent Alpha Forge garage with the name Bearings (Cardiff) Ltd being registered in 1940. Expansion plans were put on hold during the Second World War when it was heavily engaged on Admiralty contracts. The end of the war meant that expansion could finally take place with Bearings becoming one of the first post-war factories to be opened in Cardiff in 1948.

The new factory in the course of construction, 10 August 1946. Houses on Caerau Park Crescent can be seen behind the steelwork with the Western Welsh workshops in the background on the left. Local people will remember the long established weeping willow trees in front of the factory that had to make way for a recent extension. One section of the factory is given over to carburettor tuning and repairs.

Harold Wilson, the then president of the Board of Trade, at the opening of Bearings new factory on 30 January 1948. Specialists in mechanical, production and maritime engineering, Bearings today employs over fifty staff at their 20,000sqft factory. It is still a family run business, being run by Alan and Peter Vaterlaws (sons of the founder E.C. Vaterlaws).

The official opening of Bearings, 30 January 1948. George Thomas (then MP for Cardiff Central) performed the ceremony that was also broadcast by the BBC. George Thomas represented the Cardiff West constituency from 1950 to the end of his political career (see p. 104) when he became Viscount Tonypandy. He is seen behind the microphone with Mr E.C. Vaterlaws (one of the founders of the company) on his left.

Avenue Cinema, 1968. Opened in 1940 as a 'super cinema deluxe' and described by the *Cardiff and Suburban News* as, 'Ely's new monument to the films, another modern cinema for the suburbs, comfort and the best films will be the reputation of the Avenue'. The week before it closed it was showing *The Mating Game*. For many years it was a showroom for Rolls Royce and Bentley cars and is currently a video hire shop.

Addison Crescent street party, 1951. Arranged to celebrate the Festival of Britain, it attracted local MP George Thomas and his mother. George Thomas was first elected as MP for Cardiff Central at the age of thirty-six in 1945. When the new constituency of Cardiff West (which included Ely) was established in 1950 he was elected as its first MP. He went on in his political career to become Minister of State in the Welsh Office (1966), Secretary of State for Wales (1968-70) and Speaker of the House of Commons (1976).

Six

The 'Res' to Culverhouse Cross

In 1869 a new church parish, Caerau-with-Ely, was created to serve the growing population around Ely Bridge. The development of the Ely Housing Estate needed a new church to be dedicated as the Church of the Resurrection (known locally as the 'Res'). The parish was to be named GlanEly parish in honour of its major benefactor.

The laying of the foundation stone at the Church of the Resurrection by Lord Glanely on 24 January 1934. Lord Glanely had promised that he would build the church in Ely in memory of his wife, Ada Mary, who had been killed in a car crash. The church was designed by Mr Ben Roderick of Aberdare and the building contractors were E. Turner and Co., of Cardiff. In 1936 Lord Glanely gave the church the adjacent hall in memory of his only son Thomas Shandon Tatem who died at the age of seven.

Church Army Hut. Since 1925 a church army hut had been used for Sunday services as part of the Caerau with Ely parish activities and for social purposes in the week. The hut was not large enough to serve the ever increasing population of this new Ely parish and in July 1933 Revd Redvers Evans, vicar of St Davids, placed before the council plans for a new church seating 500 people and costing £5,000. The *Western Mail and Echo* headline on 13 September 1933 read: 'Lord Glanely's £10,000 gift to build a church – to replace army hut at Ely'.

A performance of the Passion play, Easter 1938. The Church of the Resurrection Passion play was performed for three nights with admission at one shilling. Participants were not allowed to openly portray Jesus.

Born at Appledore in north Devon on the 6 March 1868, Lord Glanely (see p. 55 and 118) made his fortune in shipowning. Having learnt the trade in the Cardiff office of Anning Bros, he set up his own shipping line in 1897 and got married in the same year, on the 14 September, to Ada Mary Williams of Penylan Farm, Cardiff. In 1910 he established the Tatem Steam Navigation Co. Ltd, which before the First World War operated a fleet of sixteen newly built tramp steamers. His contribution to the war effort, in which he was to lose half his fleet, gained him a knighthood and the title of Baron Glanely. Unlike many others he survived the collapse of the post-war shipping boom but was surrounded by personal tragedy, his only son dying in 1905 and his wife was killed in a car crash (see p. 105). He also died tragically, in a German bombing raid on Weston-super-Mare on 24 June 1942.

Ely Racketeers outing around 1935. The Racketeers were formed in the mid-1920s with eighteen members. A newspaper article of the time states they formed to assist charity and have 'succeeded not only in augmenting the funds of various institutions but also in giving happiness to many…the attractive costumes of brown and orange which are worn for the opening items of the programme give place later to an amusing array of garments including feather boas, hats trimmed profusely with ostrich feathers, bustles, "grannies" bonnets and other wear long since out of date for ordinary occasions are still the height of fashion when the Racketeers are working for charity'.

Hiles Road Football Club which was formed in 1930. As the name suggests lads from Hiles Road made up the team, which was captained by Mr J. Harding. Home matches were played on the old Ely recreation ground at the back of Plymouth Woods – the only pitch available at the time.

Left: Mrs Tegwedd Mary Wisbey, with 'Prince' outside 9 Howell Road, in the 1930s. She lived there with her husband Edwin James Wisbey and their son George, who was to take over the tenancy. *Right:* George Wisbey's three-year-old daughter Ann in Howell Road around 1948/9. George Wisbey was, by now, working as a plasterer (a local job had been Ely Gospel Hall on the Grand Avenue) and lived there with his wife Elizabeth, daughter Ann and son Edwin.

Myra Roberts and her brother outside Glyndwr Road in 1928.

A class photograph at Windsor Clive School in 1929. 'It will be almost like a Crystal Palace' claimed Alderman H.M. Thompson when describing Windsor Clive Open Air Council School. This was the headline in the *Western Mail* on 24 September 1928 following the foundation stone ceremony performed by the Earl of Plymouth. The Crystal Palace reference came about because of the large expanse of glass incorporated in the design. Large windows were to be fixed along one side of the classrooms with glazed folding screens that were intended to be opened during school hours. Projecting glazed roofs offered protection from the rain while admitting ultra violet rays through the special 'Vita' glass that was used throughout the school.

Windsor Clive Junior School Pageant of Peace in 1934.

The boys' teaching staff at Windsor Clive School, December 1932. The school was planned to accommodate 1,200 pupils, split as 400 boys, 400 girls and 400 infants. The contract was awarded to W.S. Eglen at a price of £22,759. The school was opened on Friday 6 September 1929 by Councillor G. Fred Evans (deputy chairman of the Education Committee and chairman of the Sites and Buildings Committee).

Windsor Clive School, champions of Division Two and winners of the Segar Cup in 1934/5.

St Francis football team. The teachers are Mr John Mahoney, Mr Gibbs and Mr J. Connor. As the Ely housing estate expanded rapidly in the 1920s many of the Roman Catholic tenants found they had neither a church nor school to cater for their needs. A centre for performing Mass was set up in Ely Hospital but by 1926 the Roman Catholic population required a more permanent base and a site was acquired on the corner of Wilson Road and Grand Avenue. Despite the hardships of that year (the year of the General Strike) the hall opened on the 10 October 1926 and St Francis became a church parish in its own right. The hall served as a heavily used parish hall changing into a church after the social events on a Saturday night. A chapel of ease was maintained in Mill Road for the Catholics of lower Ely. On the 17 October 1928 Archbishop Mostyn laid the foundation stone for a new junior school. Father Wall, who was the parish priest for over twenty years, was instrumental in planning the new St Francis parish church in south Ely that was to be built on Cowbridge Road (West). This modern post-war design with its openwork bell campanile (actually housing loudspeakers to relay the bells) was designed by F.R. Bates, Son and Price. Dedicated to St Francis of Assisi it was officially opened on Easter Tuesday 19 April 1960 by Archbishop McGrath.

A view out of the side window of Morris's stores looking up Wilson Road in the mid-1950s. Stork's shop and the St Francis church hall can be clearly seen. Other shops at this period included: Thomas & Evans Ltd (grocers), Frank Boulter, Wm.G. Murrell (greengrocer), M.J. Roberts (butcher), Miss D. O'Neil, J. Hughes (confectioner), David Lowy, Hedley J. Thomas (chemist), Parish's Stores (drapers), Shirley's ladies' hair stylist, Chas S. Morris (general grocer), F.J. Stork & Sons Ltd (newsagents, tobacconist and confectioner), Maypole Dairy Co. Ltd., Walter Boon, W.H. Poole (butcher), Gilbert Herbert, The Glendale (greengrocers), H.W. Jennings (hairdresser), Belmont Drapers, David Caple, Mrs E.B. Morris (confectioner), B. Constantine (hairdresser), Alpha Dry Cleaners, Geo.J. Mason (grocers) and Geo. Norton.

Morris's Stores in Wilson Road. The Morris family finally left Ely after thirty-five years as shopkeepers in the area.

Another view of Morris's Stores, showing a surgery upstairs and George Pyatt's drapery store next door. Morris's were one of the first three shops to open in Wilson Road. A street directory, published at the time, lists the following stores in Wilson Road: W.J. Murrell (greengrocer), W.T. Morris (grocer), W.H. Poole (butcher), H.J. Thomas (chemist), F.L. Ridd (tobacconist), F.L. Ridd (fish and chip bar), H.R. Jacob (newsagent), D.J. Roberts (butcher) and S. Glancey (grocer).

Some of the female staff who worked for the Morris family in Ely in the late 1940s. Mr Charlie Morris is on the left.

Mrs Morris and Mr Crouch in the storeroom of the Melba ice cream factory. This was situated in the basement at the rear of Morris's bakery in Highbury Place. The factory began in 1945/6 and manufactured ice cream for ten years. As well as supplying products such as choc ices, vanilla and strawberry ice cream to their own Milk Bars, the factory also supplied Woolworths.

Parish's Stores in the 1950s. Originally occupied by George Pyatt's drapery store, this shop was taken over by Parish's Stores in the 1940s. Parish's had previously owned a boot shop at the top end of Wilson Street.

Parker Place children's street party, 1945.

A 1930s view of Lewis's grocery shop at 353 Grand Avenue. The shop was owned and run by Thomas John Lewis and his wife Mary Elizabeth from 1933 until 1958. Next door was Davies's newsagent and tobacconist shop. There were two other stores – a butcher and a fish and chip shop. The photograph shows Chris Davies (shop assistant) and Mr Lewis's mother, Rachel, in the doorway and Ieuan Lewis on the pavement.

A Victory day party and procession in Meyrick Road 1945. The Queen is Mary Harris.

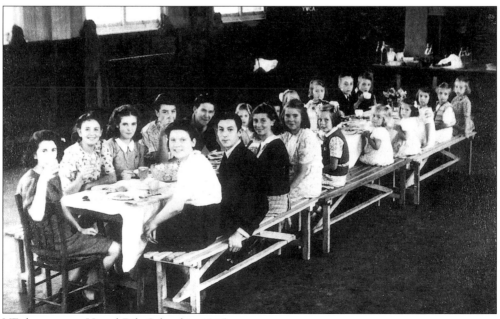

VE day party at Hywel Dda School in 1945.

'MICHAELSTON super ELY, a parish in the union of Cardiff, hundred of Dinas-Powis, county of Glamorgan, South Wales, 4½ miles (w.) from Cardiff: containing sixty inhabitants. This small parish, which derives its name from the dedication of its church to St Michael, and its distinguishing appellation from its situation on the southern bank of the river Ely, which separates it from the parish of St Fagan. [It] is beautifully situated on the south-eastern part of the country, and comprises a moderate portion of rich arable and pasture land, which is in a good state of cultivation. It was formerly distinguished for a castle erected here, probably by some of the Norman invaders of the Principality, but of which little of the history has been preserved, and scarcely the ruins are at present distinguishable. The surrounding scenery is pleasantly varied, and the distant views extend over a highly fertile and cultivated tract of country. The living is a discharged rectory, with the rectory of St Bride's super Ely consolidated, rated in the king's books at £8 6s 8d, net income, £83, patron, Llewelyn Traherne Esq. The church, dedicated to St Michael, is not remarkable for any architectural details. The total expenditure of the parochial rates for the year ending 25 March 1837, amounted to £35, of which £32 was appropriated for the relief of the poor, and £3 towards county rates.' (From A Topographical Dictionary of Wales by Samuel Lewis, London, 1840)

Drope railway viaduct, which was demolished on 24 January 1983. Built by the Barry Dock and Railway Company (later Barry Railway), it formed part of the section undertaken by the contractor Thomas A. Walker under the engineer John Wolfe Barry. The realization of the plan to build this railway had long been the ambition of David Davies MP, 'Davies the Ocean', to provide an alternative outlet to Cardiff's Bute Docks. The chimney, seen on the far right, belonged to a pump house where a steam pump drew water from a well near the viaduct. It was then pumped to Wenvoe reservoir to supply Barry Docks.

The Court, sketched by David Jones of Wallington in 17 October 1888. The Plymouth estate map of 1766 shows an L-shaped block named 'The Court' just to the left of Great House Farm. The churchwardens accounts for 1839/40 show that a William Lewis, with an income of £34 10s, paid a rate of 8s 7d for 'The Court and other lands'. The new 'Court' was built by William J. Tatem.

A postcard view of The Court in the 1920s. This is a rear view of the house looking on to its extensive lawns, much of which now forms the Glamorgan Wanderers ground. A famous resident of the new Court (now a home for the elderly) was Harry Llewellyn. As a young boy in the early 1920s, he moved with his family from Fairfield in Aberdare to The Court. He described The Court as '…a big house to accommodate our parents, eight children, a governess, nurse and eight staff…There were eight men in the garden…two in the hunting stables…and two or three others on the stud farm at Llanmaes'. The grounds had rock gardens, ponds and tennis courts where well-known players such as Betty Nuthall and Charles Kingsley played exhibition matches for charity.

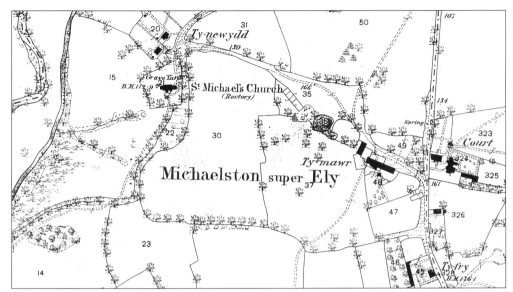

An Ordnance Survey map of Michaelston-super-Ely from 1879. Note Ty Mawr or 'Great House', a farm which stood near the present day Deepfield Close and Denison Way. In 1841 William Lougher lived at the farm with his wife, eight children and seven servants. His income was £71 5s per annum. Forty years later Richard Thomas ran the 54-acre farm with no servants suggesting a decline in the farms fortunes.

Harry Llewellyn riding 'Foxhunter' to victory in the Helsinki Olympics, 1952. Like Lord Glanely, whose house his family had acquired in the 1920s, he shared a great love of horse racing. He had been connected with horses since he was four years old and had ridden in a Grand National at the age of twenty-five, securing second place on 'Ego'. He became a national celebrity when, as Lt-Col. Henry Morton Llewellyn OBE, he was part of the 1952 Great Britain team winning a show jumping gold medal at the Helsinki Olympics. He rode many times as an amateur at Cardiff races in Ely and finished fourth in the 1933 Welsh Grand National on 'Silver Grail'. The race was won by 'Pebble Ridge' owned by Lord Glanely and trained by Ivor Anthony. In 1939, at the last race meeting in Ely, Harry Llewellyn rode 'La Petit Savoyard' to victory. He had a long association with Ely and in 1958 he became chairman of Rhymney Brewery, overseeing the acquisition of the Ely Brewery and its merger with Crosswell's to create one brewery in Ely. Col. Llewellyn was also responsible for the giant advertising sign that appeared in 1962 by the brewery facing Ely bridge. It had a considerable impact in the form of a seven-foot high tankard that filled up with a beer over and over again!

A trolleybus in Macdonald Road. Note the electric power supply feeding the overhead wires. The tram extension to Victoria Park was completed on 17 November 1904. Despite the efforts of Councillor Illtyd Thomas (of Ely Farm) to make sure that the track ran as far as the entrance to Ely Paper Mills, this plan was not adopted. Four extensions were agreed in 1927, one of which was '2 miles 9.4 chains extending the Cowbridge Road tramway from Victoria Park…for about $1\frac{1}{2}$ miles along Cowbridge Road with a bridge over the Great Western Railway main line, then turning off to the north along Grand Avenue (not yet built) as far as a point 21.5 chains west of Wilson Road'. The other three extensions went ahead but because of cost, the success of buses already running in Ely and the fact there would still be a need for a bus from Wilson Road to St Fagans Road the Ely scheme was cancelled. A trolleybus extension to Ely was begun in March 1954 and on Sunday 8 May 1955 the last new trolleybus extension in Wales began operation in Ely.

The last trolleybus run, December 1969. The decorated trolleybus is seen overtaking a motor bus on its way up Green Farm Hill just in front of the Earl Haig houses.

The bottom of Green Farm Hill in the early 1960s. Saintwell chapel can be seen on the right with a Western Welsh bus proceeding along the Cowbridge Road (West). In 1889, when Saintwell was a small but distinct area of Caerau, Mr W. Windsor began a series of cottage meetings in the area and a wooden structure was erected. As the *History of Congregationalism* points out '...the membership was entirely of the labouring class, and owing to continual removals from the locality, it was difficult to make rapid progress'. The chapel for many years was nicknamed the 'navvy church' probably because of the workers who were employed on the Wenvoe tunnel in 1888/9. Finally a sum of £80 was raised and this church was erected with an opening service taking place on 12 December 1907.

Another view of the Heol Trelai/Cowbridge Road (West) junction.

Mrs P. Howell (left) and Mrs Pittard (right) cleaning the old Saintwell chapel. Fundraising continued after the opening of the chapel and throughout the First World War which enabled the purchase of new seating and a pipe organ. In the end a further £63 1s 2d was raised for war charities. Mr Windsor, who had conducted services for twenty-nine years, had to retire through ill health and died one month later on 28 July 1918. On 26 March 1919 a service was held at Saintwell with a memorial tablet placed in the chapel in Mr Windsor's memory. In 1952, in the chapel's 60th year, the first full time minister, the Revd J.R. Hughes, was appointed. Saintwell chapel closed in the early 1960s, when a new building was erected further down Heol Trelai.

The last outing organized by the old Saintwell chapel, 23 May 1961.

Saintwell Sunday School Whitsun treat, early 1960s. This view looks up Cowbridge Road (West) towards Culverhouse Cross.

The entrance to Western Cemetery in the winter of 1957. The Western Cemetery, so named because of its position on the western edge of Cardiff, was opened in 1936. Part of the cemetery, at the corner of Cowbridge Road and Michaelston Road, contains a war memorial with graves maintained by the Imperial War Graves Commission.

Gardens behind Cowbridge Road (West) after the Second World War. In the background on the right can be seen the Culverhouse Cross hotel. This was built by Brains Brewery during the 1930s as part of a programme to modernize its public house stock and replace its smaller pubs with 'roadhouse' style establishments. It took its name from the now demolished Culverhouse Farm (which had its own dovecote or 'culverhouse') and was a replacement for the nearby Caerau Arms. The former pub, frequented by locals, such as William Thomas over two hundred years ago, is now a private house next to the Culverhouse Cross hotel.

VE day celebrations at Cyntwell.

A group photograph of the Newman family taken on an ash path pavement outside 453 Cowbridge Road (West) on 28 June 1930.

Left: Residents outside 453 Cowbridge Road (West). In the 1950s there were a number of commercial premises after the end of this terrace including Gowan Herbert Ltd, Mossford W. & Co., sculptors, First & Last Café, South Wales Caravan Distributors Ltd and Culverhouse Cross Garage. *Right:* Another view of 453 Cowbridge Road (West) this time showing younger member of the family. Note original length of gardens.

Bowmaker (Plant) Ltd, 1961. The Culverhouse Cross base of the Caterpillar dealer, Finning Ltd, is remembered for the large pieces of earthmoving plant such as giant dumper trucks and excavators that could be seen parked outside the depot. Originally opened on Tuesday 26 September 1961, the depot employed forty-three people in the workshops with fifteen office staff. Finning later moved from Ely to new purpose-built premises at Llantrisant business park which were was opened on the 30 June 1997. The Culverhouse Cross depot was not actually built by Bowmakers but by the original owner who had erected the steelwork of an ex-RAF hangar on the site. Bowmakers decided to modify the structure by removing the two front trusses and re-erecting them at the rear of the building. A two-storey steel framed office block was then erected at the front. Finning has many long serving employees including ex-Cyntwell School boys who joined in 1968: Gary Greenslade, Clive Goodall and Barry Fountain – joining Martyn Williams, who had started the year before. Bowmakers was officially opened on the 26 September 1961 and the company opened three new branches in that year, described in their literature as its '…silent salesmen'. Today the cleared site is silent and awaits redevelopment.

Caterpillar truck type 769 outside Bowmakers.

A group of Cat 785s outside the Finning depot. Standing 18ft 6in high, 21ft 10in wide and 36ft 2in long these machines had a loaded weight of 231 tons.

Wenvoe Railway tunnel vent, November 1998. The tunnel (1 mile 107 yds long) was the heaviest engineering work on the Barry Railway. Built in 1888/9 (the northern portal carries the date 1888) two special trains passed through it on the 18 July 1889 with 2,000 invited guests on their way to the official opening of Barry Dock. Today the tunnel carries large diameter water pipes and is ventilated by one 15ft diameter shaft. The circular brick stack shown here, at the rear of the Brooklands Terrace retail park, is seen in the process of being demolished and replaced by a modern structure.

Culverhouse Cross site (A), one of the four principal out-of-town retail locations in Cardiff is Culverhouse Cross, in the mid-1980s. This location, originally based on the Tesco foodstore and Marks & Spencer department store (indicated by the white lined area in the photograph), has seen two recent additions. These included the Wenvoe Retail Park (Castlemore) and more recently Brooklands Terrace (Davies Street Properties in conjunction with Standard Life). The rental for the largest of the units there is in excess of half a million pounds per year! While most local people feel that the location has long exceeded saturation point in terms of road traffic there is news that United News & Media have submitted a planning application to develop the existing HTV Studios for retail and leisure use.

Site map (B) of Culverhouse Cross. This site map, produced by the former South Glamorgan County Council in the mid-1980s, shows the development at that time around Culverhouse Cross – the recently completed HTV Studios and the uncompleted link road can be seen but not the Copthorne Hotel, Tesco or Marks & Spencer stores. The white lined area, adjoining the Cambrian Caravan Park, has been developed for housing as 'Parc yr Gwenfo'. Note the open fields around Culverhouse Cross!